Thinking at the Crossroads

A Buddhist Exploration of Western Thought

Advayacitta

Nagadhatu Publishing

Published by Nagadhatu Publishing

ISBN 978-0-9956870-0-4

A catalogue record for this book is available from the British Library.

ACKNOWLEDGEMENTS

My warm thanks go to all who have made comments on the draft essays in this book, and in particular to Punyamala, Sthirananda, and Alice Bartlett, for their help in preparing it for publication.

CONTENTS

PREFACE

The essays in this book are concerned with the nature of ideas, and especially how ideas affect human behaviour for good or ill. They explore influential aspects of Western thought and the consequences these have had, both beneficial and harmful. They also explore how thinking in the future might develop, especially when considering the interaction between Buddhism and the best in Western thought.

The essays are written to stimulate others to consider the vital importance of ideas and beliefs in shaping their own and other people's behaviour. They are also written to help protect the positive developments in Western thought, and the beneficial practices associated with them.

I am very conscious that in many ways the essays are preliminary, and that to some extent their style reflects the set of talks I gave, upon which they are based. Much more could be written on the topics I address. However, in publishing these essays I am concerned to encourage others to think about the issues discussed within them.

Advayacitta

Thinking at the Crossroads

1

Ideas and Beliefs

The Western world is now experiencing a profound crisis. Many people have become thoroughly disillusioned with Western politics, especially as politicians seem to make a mess of just about everything they do. Mainstream politicians appear incapable of providing anything other than a combination of old ideological clichés and sound-bite inanities. They also appear to have become a privileged class, distanced from most of their electorates, and too influenced by powerful interest groups. Indeed, western democracy has been described as having become 'hollowed out' (1), with mainstream political parties no longer in any real sense representing the interests of the great majority of people that vote for them. This has led to the rise of what have been called 'populist' politicians and parties.

Furthermore, although there has been moderate economic recovery, at least in some countries, there are persistent major effects of the financial crisis of 2007-8. Unemployment, especially amongst the young, is in many countries very high. This has not been helped by the effects of globalisation, with the demise of old industries in various Western countries. Also, the future stability of the world economy is far from guaranteed. This economic malaise has contributed to many people's disenchantment with traditional politics.

Ironically this situation has come about twenty-five years or so after the fall of soviet communism, which for many people heralded the victory and superiority of Western liberal democracy. One author had even called this the 'end of history', meaning the culminating point of human social and political development in liberal democracy (2). He was making an ironic contrast to Marxists' previous use of that phrase, with their belief that communism would achieve that 'end', or supposed culmination. But he has been proven as wrong as the Marxists. The fall of soviet communism is lamented by few, with its record of mass murder and concentration camps standing as a chilling reminder of what it was really like, and as a conclusive indictment of what belief in Marxism actually entails in practice. Yet the victory of the West in the 'cold war' seems to have brought few rewards to the West, apart from a respite from the threat of nuclear war.

In Europe, in particular, the crisis has also brought into question the existence of the European Union, a political entity which, whatever its merits, has undermined national sovereignty and democratic processes, and, through allowing mass immigration into member states, has eroded many people's sense of security, as well as their sense of belonging to a country that is in some way their own. Yet in the background is the memory of the appalling harm ethnic nationalism, especially in its Nazi form, brought to Europe and the rest of the world in the twentieth century.

In general, in the West there is a lack of serious, new political thinking. There seems to be nothing except for old political clichés which now appear very inadequate, and which have all been proven wanting. Even the 'green' movement appears to offer little but old political ideas dressed up in environmentalist clothing. Nevertheless, there are still those who cling to one type of political belief or another, vociferously denouncing the views of others of a different political persuasion. Few, if any, recognise the underlying assumptions common to themselves and their opponents, and whilst they are quick to spot the flaws in their opponents' beliefs they are typically blind to the flaws in their own.

These flaws go right across the political spectrum. At their worst, in ideologies such as Marxism, Nazism and ethnic nationalism, the negative aspects of Western thought have been shown to be appalling in their effects, which have included two world wars, the cold war, and the deaths of over a hundred million people at the hands of their own governments. But the harmful effects were not just due to those extreme ideologies.

Another system of ideas from the Western tradition, neo-classical economics - the theory underlying unregulated 'free market' economic practice - has also been shown to lead to harm, through mass financial idiocy and an economic parasitism that extracts profits from companies with little regard for the companies themselves, the well-being of the people working in them, the local societies in which they are situated, or the world as a whole. This particular theory was the major ideological factor in the development of the financial crisis of the last decade (in tandem with the basic human failing of greed).

Yet it must not be forgotten, or unacknowledged, that the West's economic system has produced much benefit as well as harm, especially at the times it was not dominated by neo-classical economic thought and practice. However, of most crucial importance is the fact that the West has been the cradle of highly important positive ideas, such as democracy and liberty, as well as the practices associated with them, practices which to some extent or other became accepted aspects of functioning Western countries. Thus Western nations, although far from perfect, have been at the forefront of the practices associated with democratic government, the liberty of the individual, and human rights.

However, these and other positive practices of the Western tradition now appear to be under threat, and the ideas upon which they are based seem to be unsupported by any current political or other philosophy that does not have its faults or weaknesses.

Indeed, these ideas and practices have also been undermined by another common political dynamic, which is best described as 'inverted prejudice'. This is often involved when activists work against specific prejudices, such as sexism and racism. As such it appears to be related to ideals of human rights, fairness and equality. Unfortunately, it has its own similar prejudices to those against which it explicitly works. Thus, those with inverted prejudice typically fight sexism against women with arguments and practices which are sexist against men. Another example is the use of the term 'racism' only to apply to white people's prejudice and discrimination against non-white people, rather than to all ethnic prejudice and discrimination by whatever ethnic groups. A similar type of inverted prejudice is the willingness of many people to criticise anything western (and, implicitly, related to white people) with which they disagree, whilst labelling any criticism of harmful non-Western beliefs and practices as being 'racist'. Inverted prejudice is characterised by double standards, and the ideals to which it is superficially related are thereby seriously weakened in many people's consideration.

The precarious position of the West leads to the question as to whether anything could be done to protect and revitalise positive Western ideas, as well as the institutions and practices which developed from them. Whatever the complex set of circumstances that have brought the West to its current position, it seems of crucial importance that its positive ideas receive serious support, and that the positive practices stemming from them are protected and strengthened.

In these essays I will be exploring aspects of Western thought from a Buddhist perspective, especially aspects of Western thought that have developed in the last few hundred years, since the rise of science. I will be arguing that the positives in Western thought have very interesting and close parallels with the essentials of Buddhist thought. One could put it that there is a close affinity between the best in Western thought and the teaching of the Buddha. Moreover, the negatives in Western thought and practice can also be clearly understood when one applies a Buddhist critique.

By 'Buddhist' here I do not mean the old institutionalised forms of Asian Buddhism but the essence of the Buddha's teaching itself, which is about truths which can be discovered anywhere that conditions are conducive. This teaching is a profound statement about the nature of reality and its implications for human life. It has nothing intrinsically to do with eastern cultures, except insofar as they have at any point successfully expressed or embodied it. It can be expressed and practised within modern western cultures, perhaps more so than within those traditional eastern ones. I consider that this is because of the affinities that exist between the Buddha's teaching and the best in western thought and practice.

It is a teaching that involves certain core principles. There are three of these which I particularly wish to emphasise. Very importantly, there is the core principle of Buddhist ethics. To put it briefly, Buddhist ethics is about the expression and cultivation of compassion, and the motivations and emotions associated with that, as well as the avoidance of whatever causes harm to oneself or others. It is about the development and expression of ethical states of mind and the behaviour arising from them.

It is crucial to understand that Buddhist ethics is a 'natural' ethics, by which I mean that, according to Buddhist teaching, human actions, and in particular human motivations, have a natural ethical or moral dimension to them, whether we know it or not. This is very different from a popular contemporary idea that ethics or morals are merely the matters of opinion of different cultural groups, and are just things that people decide without there being any naturally existing morality to human behaviour and motivation. This modern belief can be termed 'relativism'.

The Buddhist understanding of the existence of natural ethics also contrasts with theistic ideas of there being moral laws set by a god. This can be called a 'revealed law' theory of ethics, with the ethical laws being seen as rules set by a god and revealed by him to human beings. Typically these supposed ethical laws have been the rules of the tribal societies which adopted the belief in a creator god (who just so happened to be their tribal deity). However, and very importantly, theism also has a 'natural law' tradition, in which there are believed to exist natural laws within the world, i.e. laws that exist within the nature of the universe, although put there by the god. Thus a crucial aspect of such theistic 'natural law' thinking is the belief that there exist natural moral laws built into the fabric of the universe by the creator god.

Strictly, one could call this theistic 'natural law' tradition more a 'semi-natural' tradition. It relies on believing that there is a creator god who imbues the universe with 'laws'. It does not really recognise that there could be a natural morality that is *fully natural*, i.e. that there exists a natural moral dimension to human motivation and actions that stems from the nature of the universe, particularly the nature of consciousness, and which does not stem from the actions of a supposed creator god. In contrast, Buddhism emphasises that there exists a natural ethical dimension to our motivation, and to what we do, that is not a matter of opinion, not culturally determined, and not determined by a hypothetical creator god.

The second core principle is that of *pratitya samutpada*, or 'conditionality'. This is the principle, taught by the Buddha, that all phenomena mutually condition each other – that they are inter-related in highly complex ways, and arise, persist and fade away in a very complex network of relationships. *Pratitya samutpada* was applied by the Buddha himself primarily to the network of psychological and ethical factors influencing human well-being, so that people could develop increasingly positive mental states through understanding what factors conditioned such states and engaging in practices which bring them about. However, it can also be understood as a general principle. Stated as a general principle it may seem very abstract, but it has profound implications.

Pratitya samutpada literally means 'arising together due to a cause', although as a principle it is subtly different from a doctrine of 'causality'. As a general principle it is indeed *very* general. The implication of this is that when studying any particular aspects of the universe, whether physical, mental, social, or whatever, one has to identify what actual phenomena there are and then empirically investigate the patterns of conditionality involving them. So *pratitya samutpada* is a rationale, if not the fundamental rationale, for empirical investigation – and hence for science - a rationale which assumes that phenomena mutually influence or condition each other. It is different from a doctrine of causality in that it is less deterministic, and allows for the possibility that with different conditions then the patterns of mutual influence will be different. So it differs from the idea of 'universal laws'. Although in many ways it is similar to such a notion, one could say that it is more 'open'.

The third core principle is that of '*śunyata*' or 'emptiness' – the principle that no phenomenon has an intrinsic, substantial nature of its own. The principle of *śunyata* implies that it is not just that phenomena are inter-related, but that it is mistaken to conceive of any specific phenomenon as existing in itself, independently of other phenomena. The principle of emptiness is a deeper aspect of the principle of conditionality. In other words, the principle of conditionality implies not just that phenomena are or become inter-related within specific systems of interaction but that no specific phenomenon exists 'in itself' somehow independently of all systems or all other phenomena.

In Buddhism, the doctrine of *śunyata* is applied principally to oneself, where it is referred to as the doctrine of *anatman*, or 'not-self'. This implies that each of us is a changing network of phenomena, mental and physical, and that each of us does not possess an inherent existence unrelated to other phenomena. In Buddhism, it is also recognised that each of us, typically and implicitly, lives under the illusion that, on the contrary, he or she does have an inherent existence as a separate, unchanging self, soul or ego. In contrast, the doctrine of *anatman* implies that each of us is an ever-changing stream of mental and physical phenomena.

Furthermore, the natural existence of morality is related to the nature of consciousness and the existence of the illusion of selfhood, the illusion that each of us is an inherently existing separate entity. Consciousness involves the experience of pleasure and pain. Within Buddhism it is recognised that unethical actions typically lead to harm, to pain and suffering for self and others, whilst ethical actions typically contribute to the well-being of self and others. Moreover, and very importantly, unethical actions are those based upon motivation that reflects or maintains the illusion that one is a separate fixed self; in contrast, ethical actions and motivation undermine that illusion or are expressions of a mental state from which the illusion has gone. Therefore Buddhist ethical principles are intimately related to those of *pratitya samutpada* and *śunyata*.

Usually the terms which Buddhists use for ethical and unethical motivation and behaviour are translated into English as 'skilful' and 'unskilful' respectively, and there are reasons for this usage (especially the need to distinguish such ethics from ideas of 'moral law'). In these essays, however, I shall employ the more usual Western terms. One particular implication of the Buddhist understanding of ethics is that selfish actions, although they may provide temporary gain to the person committing them, are also nevertheless harmful to that person. The natural, over-riding consequence of actions based upon the illusion of separate selfhood, is suffering for self and others. One aspect of this is that unethical motivation and actions intensify the illusion of selfhood, 'congealing the ego' as it were, and thereby lead to restricted mental states from which deeper happiness is excluded.

Very importantly, there is an ethical dimension to ideas. In other words, ideas, and systems of ideas, can be expressions of moral or immoral motivation, and can reinforce and encourage such motivation. In particular, they can be expressions of particular emotional impulses associated with the ego-illusion, such as hatred and craving. For example, systems of ideas like those of Nazism and Communism, which focus upon, exaggerate and invent the harm done by a particular group of people, and which dehumanise those people, are potent expressions of hatred. Economic theories can be expressions of craving, through rationalising behaviour stemming from greed.

Ideas can also reinforce the ego-illusion in that they explicitly build a strong fixed sense of identity, to which one becomes very attached, for example the belief that one 'is' a member of a special group. Moreover, one's ego, one's sense of self, can be bound up with any ideas to which one has become very attached, not just those which explicitly bolster a specific sense of identity. These ideas can also become an implicit part of one's sense of identity. Political beliefs are major examples of both explicit and implicit attachment to ideas.

People often explicitly identify themselves strongly with being 'a socialist' or 'a conservative', or as being 'left wing' or 'right wing'. Alongside this, they often hold firmly to beliefs which are expressions of that politicised identity, no matter what evidence there is against such beliefs. As examples, people can be firmly attached to beliefs such as 'equality' or 'the free market', despite evidence against them. Indeed, a typical feature of such attachment to ideas is the process of distortion of evidence, often through someone being highly selective in what evidence they consider. The attachment to having a particular political identity is also typically accompanied by a marked tendency to identify people who disagree with one's political views as being of an opposite, supposedly negative and inferior identity. This is often accompanied by a focus upon what is wrong with the other person's opinions and actions, with a corresponding disregard of the faults in one's own.

Mention of such distortion of evidence brings us to another aspect of the ego-illusion, which is *delusion*. By the term 'delusion' in this context I mean holding firmly onto a belief that is actually significantly contradicted by evidence, in other words being attached to a belief which does not correspond to the actual nature of the universe or some specific aspects of it.

In general, from a Buddhist perspective, ideas are ethically highly important. For people who have committed themselves to the Buddhist spiritual path it is vitally important to recognise the ideas they hold, and to come to recognise the effects of those ideas on themselves and others. So it is crucial for Buddhists to become aware of the attachment they have to any ideas, and to come to understand how this distorts their consideration of evidence, as well as to recognise what emotional and ethical factors are involved in those ideas and attachment to them. However, this can be generalised to non-Buddhists: it is vital for anyone to become aware of the ideas they hold, and of the actual effects of those ideas, to ensure their own and others' well-being.

What then is an 'idea'? One dictionary definition is as follows: 'any product of mental apprehension or activity, existing in the mind as an object of knowledge or thought; a thought, conception, notion; an item of knowledge or belief' (3). So an idea is a concept, or a specific aspect of knowledge or belief. Examples could be the idea of 'tree', or 'free market', or 'god', or 'sub-atomic particle', or 'society'. Ideas can be of very many varieties, from all areas of human activity and understanding. Perhaps one could put it that ideas are the building blocks of understanding. Moreover, they can be combined into systems of thought, which one can refer to as 'idea systems' and 'belief systems'.

By the term 'idea system' I refer to any particular, relatively coherent set of ideas about the world or some aspect of the world, a set of ideas actually used by individual people. By 'coherent' I do not mean logically coherent (although they might be). Rather I mean a set of ideas which people actually hold, and which somehow collectively form an entity, if only because people use them associated together. Idea systems tend to be made of sets of specific component ideas, although the components can change, at least to some extent, over time. An idea system may possess a structure, in the way that its component ideas relate to each other. One can perhaps identify 'core ideas' which are the main aspects of an idea system, and subsidiary ideas which stem from those core ideas, or support them in some way. Some idea systems may themselves be the components of larger idea systems.

Idea systems are ways human beings classify and try to understand the world or aspects of it, and which they use to guide their actions within it. They can derive from a variety of sources - scientific, religious, philosophical, cultural and political, amongst others. (People can of course also learn and understand idea systems without using them to make decisions or act, if they consciously do not agree with the ideas.)

Then there are what I call 'belief systems'. With this term I refer to an idea system which is held with a strong conviction of its correctness, which is concerned with important aspects of the world, and which relates, in at least some crucial ways, poorly to the evidence from the actual world. Belief systems may be comprised of sets of political views, religious beliefs, philosophical ideas, and cultural beliefs, amongst other things. Importantly, a belief system may contain ideas which contradict each other, but which nevertheless are jointly believed. Indeed, the inner contradictions of a belief system can have a psychological effect, making people more defensive when the beliefs are criticised, because to some extent they are aware of the contradictions. The contradictions can also bring about confused thinking.

There is no clear dividing line between idea systems and belief systems. By the former I mean a coherent set of ideas. By the latter I mean a set of ideas which is significantly contradicted by evidence, but which is nevertheless believed in strongly. An alternative term for a belief system is an ideology.

Whatever the system of ideas we use, there is also the question of how well we use it. On the one hand, we can use ideas very logically. We have developed systems of logic, and of mathematics, as well as various scientific conceptual systems. In the practice of law there can also be great attention to evidence and what logical inferences can be drawn from it. On the other hand, very often we are not very logical in our thinking. There seems to be a natural human default option of what one could call 'emotive thinking'. This is thinking influenced by emotions, and by other factors such as the situation we are in. This is unsurprising. Our distant ancestors had to make decisions quickly, for example when running from a wild animal that was attacking them. That is not a situation in which one has the leisure to think through the various options in a logical fashion. One has to make decisions fast, based upon a quick appraisal of available evidence, with fear a motivating factor.

Moreover, our ideas can be used illogically in a variety of ways. One way, which I mentioned above, is simply by ignoring evidence against the idea being true. This is often because the possibility that the idea is false is too threatening to contemplate. Another way we can be illogical is by believing simultaneously in two ideas that seriously contradict each other.

Ideas pass from person to person, and from group to group. They can be spread in many different ways. We can actively teach them, or they can be passed on as implicit assumptions underlying what we say or do. The spread of ideas is also dependent upon technology; for example, the internet has increased access to ideas. Before the internet we were dependent upon books and libraries, or direct person to person contact (whether in a formal teaching situation or informal). Furthermore, once there were no books. Ideas could then spread only much more slowly. Indeed, the invention of printing appears to have been a very important development for the human race, in particular because it allowed ideas to spread much faster than before.

Ideas can not only be actively spread but can also be suppressed. This can happen when they challenge someone's authority or position, for example that of an authoritarian government, or when they challenge accepted beliefs, especially religious beliefs.

There is a useful analogy when considering ideas, although it should not be taken too far. This is that ideas, and the propagation of ideas, can be compared to computer software and its dissemination. In many ways the ideas we hold are responsible for, or strongly influence, what we do, feel and think – just as computer software programmes determine what computers do. Computer software can be downloaded from computer to computer, and ideas pass from person to person. There are differences however, in that ideas, and systems of ideas, are learned and internalised by people relatively slowly, usually through some process of gradual acquisition, whereas computer software can be downloaded in an instant and the computer does not have to go through a laborious process of learning. Also, people can persistently understand concepts poorly as well as apply them badly, whereas computer software usually has most of its faults removed before it is widely propagated. People also have inherent attributes that are a result of our evolutionary history, and there are complex interactions between systems of ideas and such inherent attributes. Some idea systems can reinforce particular inherited traits, which in turn can lead to increasing the strength with which those ideas are believed. At other times inherited traits, or even simply acquired habits, can over-ride the ideas we believe in, and lead to actions which go against those ideas.

The computer analogy is important if one asks the question 'how do people understand a given situation and act within it?' Whilst people can be inconsistent, make basic mistakes, and at times act more or less instinctively, the specific idea systems they have learned and internalised form a dominant part of what guides their actions. Particularly important are belief systems which are dominant in their culture and society, and which thereby have acquired a certain apparent legitimacy. People can act upon such beliefs, with the further belief that they are acting correctly in doing so. Indeed, it can be inconceivable to people that the generally accepted belief system may be wrong. Unfortunately such beliefs and actions can lead to much harm.

It is also the case that people can hold ideas without explicitly knowing they do. Idea systems may be passed on and picked up automatically, rather like the way a child unconsciously learns the rules of language when it learns to speak – nobody explicitly teaches it, but its brain learns to recognise the patterns within speech, and to copy them.

There is a certain irony here, in that ideas may not necessarily be consciously held, but are nevertheless reflected in behaviour – we have ideas but do not know it. Such patterns can come from influential ideas that have become generally accepted within a culture, but which are no longer necessarily explicitly emphasised. They are more like implicit assumptions underlying people's thinking and behaviour. The economist John Maynard Keynes wrote: *"The ideas of economists and political philosophers, both when they are right and when they are wrong, are more powerful than is commonly understood. Indeed the world is ruled by little else. Practical men who believe themselves to be quite exempt from any intellectual influence are usually the slaves of some defunct economist. Madmen in authority who hear voices in the air are distilling their frenzy from some academic scribbler of years back"* (4).

Extending the computer software metaphor, idea systems, and especially belief systems, can also be at times like computer viruses, passing from person to person and subverting healthy functioning in doing so.

Of course, the use of the term 'virus' in computing is itself metaphorical, coming from the discipline of biology. In this regard it is interesting that nineteenth century neurologists and psychiatrists, such as Jean-Martin Charcot and Pierre Janet, in their work on hysteria, hypothesised that there could be unconscious factors within the mind that could act like 'viruses' or 'parasites', subverting normal psychological functioning. Charcot wrote the following about ideas planted through suggestion: *"an idea, a coherent group of ideas settle themselves in the mind in the fashion of parasites, remaining isolated from the rest of the mind and expressing themselves outwardly through corresponding motor phenomena. The group of suggested ideas finds itself isolated and cut off from the control of that large collection of personal ideas accumulated from a long time, which constitutes consciousness proper, that is the Ego"* (5).

He was referring to hysteria in particular. The 'suggestion' to which he is referring is not deliberate hypnotic suggestion but the unconscious process through which we may respond to any implicit suggestions in what people say or do.

Pierre Janet called such phenomena 'subconscious fixed ideas' and stated: *"The idea, like a virus, develops in a corner of the personality - inaccessible to the subject, works subconsciously, and brings about all disorders of hysteria and mental disease."* (6)

Charcot and Janet were referring to the effects of quite specific ideas affecting individuals' mental health. However, one could put it that an idea system is like a virus, or computer virus, when it takes over a person's mind so that their thinking and behaviour are, at least at times, dominated by it, either to their own harm or to the harm of others.

Now ideas do not exist in a vacuum. Ideas are held by human beings. Moreover, although I have used the metaphor of computer software, people are not computers. So what then are human beings?

We are a mammalian species, 'homo sapiens sapiens', and in particular we evolved from the ape family, and are genetically closely related to chimpanzees. We are a species in which intelligence evolved increasingly, especially over the last hundred and fifty thousand years. Thus we are intelligent apes. Also, we typically exist in groups, whether small or large. We lived, until the development of agriculture, as groups of hunter gatherers. One could perhaps call chimpanzees, and many other animals, 'hunter gatherers', as they gather foods and also to some extent or other hunt other animals. However, there is the very important difference with humans in that our ancestors made increasingly sophisticated tools, which gave them definite advantages in staying alive and propagating their species. Whilst some animals, such as chimpanzees, can prepare and make rudimentary use of natural objects as simple tools, it is human beings alone who have developed increasingly complex tools, and who have used those tools to make other articles.

For whatever complex set of factors, our species became increasingly intelligent and skilled, in a variety of ways. We evolved highly increased dexterity, with developed abilities to make ever more complex and sophisticated tools and other articles. We evolved artistic and musical abilities. Crucially, we developed sophisticated language and thinking skills – including the ability to form concepts and ideas. Furthermore, we developed the capacity to be cooperative with each other, an attribute which is associated with our living in groups. But humans are also a violent species. We kill and physically harm other animals, and also each other.

Let us consider our species as it would have been during that long prehistoric period of being hunter gatherers. Let us assume that a particular group of humans was hunting and gathering reasonably successfully, but suppose that another such human group came along. The danger was a very real one that the other group would take the food, thereby threatening the first group's survival. What then could the first group do? Perhaps do what chimpanzees do, try to kill as many members of the other group as possible. It is of note that this is how chimpanzee groups can behave. Whether we have inherited our violent tendencies from a common ancestor to humans and chimpanzees, or whether such tendencies evolved independently in us and chimpanzees, there is nevertheless a dilemma when a hunter-gatherer group encounters another such group. The dilemma, which I will term the 'fundamental dilemma', is whether to kill or risk the possibility of either losing one's food supply or being killed by the other group.

There were perhaps some ways for such groups to develop a truce or non-violent relationship with each other, possibly increasingly so as our ancestors grew more intelligent and less rigidly driven by instincts. Yet, in such circumstances, to trust each other is not so easy, especially when food is scarce. Moreover, in that hunter gatherer environment, the more successful one was at fighting, the more likely one was to survive and pass on one's DNA to the next generation. So, unfortunately there is likely to have been a selection process at work that favours violence. Given such a crucial issue in our evolutionary history, it is unsurprising that we are a violent animal.

Could human beings learn to overcome this legacy of evolution? In particular, given our evolutionary history, certain questions arise - would it be possible for such an animal to overcome violence, to feel secure without it, and also ensure that every member of the species gets enough to eat? Is it at all possible for human beings to overcome the fundamental dilemma?

There is still much violence and poverty in the world. However, we have made progress in both areas, despite the impression many people have that this is not the case. Actually the percentage of the human population harmed by violence is much lower now than it was in hunter gatherer times, or compared to any other time in history, and in recent years the percentage of the world population experiencing real poverty has decreased significantly. Nevertheless there is a long way to go, and there is no guarantee that we will not lose what we have gained. Can we progress further?

As I mentioned, we became very good at making tools and articles, for hunting, fighting, and many other tasks. Furthermore, the better we got at making things, the more we transformed our world. It became easier to get food, and the human population increased. Our language skills and many other abilities developed further. Nevertheless, it is evident that the fundamental dilemma continued, with neighbouring groups, over the millennia growing larger, being explicit or implicit threats to each other, a situation which has persisted down to the present day. I acknowledge that I am presenting here a dark picture of our evolutionary history, and it is of importance to note that the very idea of evolution has itself been politicised, with grave consequences, as I will discuss in my fourth chapter.

But we *are* intelligent. In particular, we are creatures who have ideas and who use those ideas to think about the world, to understand it, or try to understand it, and to act upon that understanding. We have developed ideas, and systems of ideas, for trying to understand, influence, and, to some extent, control human behaviour itself. What is very evident is that some of those ideas, and systems of ideas and beliefs, have exacerbated human negativity, whilst others have helped the expression of human positivity. Can we develop the ideas that will enable us to further cultivate our positivity as well as overcome our negativity so that the human race can survive and prosper through this century and into the next? Or will our ideas, and their effects on the human and natural worlds, exacerbate our negativity and outrun our ability to constrain any harm done?

2

Central Aspects of the Western Tradition

The ideas I will be exploring here are ones that significantly inform modern Western thought. Historically they are associated with the rise of science in the context of Christianity, as well as the re-emergence of classical Greco-Roman thought from the early Renaissance onwards. The history of Western ideas is bound up with the interplay between Christianity, classical thought and science. I will be looking at specific ideas that are associated with this.

Thus there are three important factors in the development of Western thought which I wish to emphasise. The first is Christianity, which became more or less the only religion in Europe, and therefore the context in which later developments occurred. The second is the revival of classical Roman and Greek thought, from the early Renaissance onwards, which helped bring about the conditions both for the rise of science and the further development of Christian thought, amongst other consequences. (Of the latter, in particular there was the rise of Renaissance humanism, and also 'natural law' thinking, both of which profoundly affected Christianity.) Thirdly there was the rise of science, with its emphasis upon empirical study of the world, rather than relying upon accepted texts.

Firstly, let us turn to the context, Christianity, and in particular to the ideas within it. What are the main ideas in Christian thought? To answer this question it is useful to ask another - what is Christianity? One aspect of the answer to that second question is that it is in part a Middle Eastern tribal religion. It derives from Judaism and stems from worship of a tribal deity, Jehovah. Also, if one studies the Old Testament one finds that this is very much to do with the unification of ancient Middle Eastern tribes under one tribal god. What is emphasised there is 'belief' in that god, and doing what that god says.

So there exists a kernel to Christianity of tribal religion. With this in mind we need to consider our hunter gatherer ancestors and the problem they had of how to respond to other groups, the 'fundamental dilemma'. The tribes of the ancient Middle East would have had similar issues with which to contend – how does one deal with the explicit or implicit threats from other tribes? One way for a tribe to make itself more secure is to form, if it can, trustworthy alliances with other tribes. But what would make such alliances more secure, more trustworthy? Maybe if all the tribes in the alliance were united in the worship of one tribal god. And, of course, that is what happened with the ancient tribes of Israel – they united under one tribal deity, Jehovah.

But there was a further development. The ancient Jewish tribes did not only unite under one deity, but they also came to see that deity as not just one tribal god among many, but as the *only* god. Thus they developed a monotheistic religion. Furthermore, Judaism's development was influenced by the Jewish experience of empires not that far away from them (in Egypt, Persia and Babylon). So the idea of there being just one god developed with some 'imperial' assumptions attached to it. Central to these are the ideas that the one god created the universe and that he rules it rather like an emperor.

Then Israel became part of the Roman Empire. There developed in fact a sizeable Jewish diaspora throughout the Roman Empire. In that empire, whose religions contained many gods, people began to consider seriously the idea of there being but one god. In this context Judaism became quite influential (1). However it was an offshoot of Judaism, Christianity, which took hold. An important point to realise is that Christianity, from its inception, was a religion of the Roman Empire. This would have reinforced the 'imperial' characteristics of the presumed one god, who was in effect imagined as a cosmic Roman emperor.

Such a conception of an all-powerful, as well as all-knowing, god has certain psychological implications. On the one hand, such a god is to be feared, especially as the ordinary human being is believed to be punished by him for disobedience – and punished eternally. On the other hand, there can be, at least at times, a significant underlying egotism associated with being a 'believer', which can make one special. Fear of a god's punishment for disobeying him, combined with arrogant righteousness for believing and obeying, is a powerful combination that has all too often led to intolerance, hatred and violence towards non-believers.

But Christianity's conception of its god is not just that of a tribal deity turned into cosmic emperor. There is the central importance of Jesus. There are two aspects to this. First there is the mythology of Jesus, as god and son of god, who is claimed to have died for people's 'sins', and who is thus a sort of ritual sacrifice or scapegoat. The second aspect is his teaching, especially that in the Sermon on the Mount. This is what one could call the teaching of 'love thy neighbour', and Jesus is himself seen as embodying the love and compassion which he teaches. From a Buddhist perspective this is an echo of the Buddha's teachings on *metta* and *karuna* – love and compassion. Importantly, such teaching is radically different from that of the Old Testament, which is very much about 'an eye for an eye' and the infliction of violence upon either tribal enemies or non-believers.

So Christianity has at heart a mixture of conflicting ideas - about its deity, and about moral behaviour. Its deity is an amalgam of tribal deity, cosmic emperor, ritual sacrifice, and god of love. Its prescriptions on morality reflect that conflicting mix, with commandments to love others juxtaposed with Old Testament incitements to violently oppose non-believers.

Christianity developed very quickly in the Roman Empire, which was actually quite tolerant of different religions. For reasons which appear unclear, Christians came to be persecuted, maybe because they refused to acknowledge the imperial gods, or maybe because their beliefs and behaviour were actually threatening to others, or perceived to be so (2).

Nevertheless Christianity grew in popularity until it was very widespread, taken up by many in the Roman Empire. Then, with its official adoption by the emperor Constantine, it became politically dominant. It subsequently drove out the original pagan religions of the Roman Empire, often violently, particularly under the reign of the emperor Theodosius (3). It developed into an authoritarian, if not totalitarian, religion. This development was exemplified in the person of Augustine. He emphasised the idea that the whole of society should be totally involved with Christian ideas and institutions. He also stressed the importance of not being tolerant towards people who differed in religion, whether they were pagans or supposed heretics. He supported and encouraged the persecution of such people. For Augustine, Christianity should be synonymous with society, and people compelled to be believers (4).

In the following centuries Christianity spread through Europe, and beyond the Roman Empire. For nearly a millennium and a half it came to dominate Western thought. On the whole Christianity was intolerant of difference, with Augustine's influential ideas reinforcing this. There evolved much later, however, especially from the time of the Renaissance humanists, a growing tolerance, although this evolution was set back for a while with the Reformation and Counter-Reformation.

The Roman Empire itself divided, with the Catholic Church coming to dominate in the western empire and the Orthodox Church in the eastern. The Western Roman Empire disintegrated, although it was later partly revived in the 'Holy Roman Empire', especially under Charlemagne. Moreover Europe, particularly Western Europe, entered what has been called the 'dark ages', otherwise known as the early medieval period.

An important question to ask is this: with the rise, political success and dominance of Christianity, what happened to the legacy of classical pagan culture? In particular, what happened to its vigorous philosophical tradition, including the works of people such as Plato and Aristotle, amongst others?

It is salutary to realise that classical pagan thought was very much actively suppressed under Christianity, especially when it first became dominant in the Roman Empire. There was, for example, the deliberate destruction of libraries. In Alexandria the library of Serapis was destroyed at the orders of the archbishop in 391. According to some, Rome itself was completely devoid of books by the middle of the fourth century, especially with the closure of its twenty-nine libraries (5). In the fourth century, in the eastern empire, because of the persecution of pagan practices by the emperor Valens, 'owners of books, through fear of a like fate, burned their entire libraries, so great was the terror that had seized upon all' (6).

Nevertheless, some classical pagan thought survived, although it tended to be used to reinforce the Christian belief system, for example, Plato's theory of archetypal forms was used to reinforce the Christian emphasis on the importance of the world beyond this one. (Plato's theory had stressed the supposed superior reality of archetypal forms, compared to the phenomena of this world.) Also, against the general trend of suppression of classical thought, some people did try to preserve classical texts and classical authors. For example, in Constantinople, under the persuasion of the scholar Themistius, there was set up a small scriptorium in which works by various classical authors were preserved and copied. These authors included Plato and Aristotle. Moreover, elsewhere in the Christian world there were others who preserved classical texts. The 'Latin transmitters' is the epithet for some of these. One such, Boethius, was executed before finishing his task of fully translating the works of Plato and Aristotle.

Another was Cassiodorus, who established a library. Thanks to these translators, and others, a proportion of classical texts survived in monastic libraries, and some classical thought survived and was studied (7). However it is also likely that many classical texts did not survive simply because they were not considered important enough to copy, preference being given to Christian works. It must be remembered that books had to be repeatedly copied in order to survive as the decades and centuries passed. Paper had not been invented nor spread to Europe. Books had to be on papyrus, and when this became difficult to obtain, parchment.

It is worthwhile to consider how little access to ideas people had in the early Middle Ages under the Catholic Church. Firstly, Augustine had emphasised the importance of faith over reason, so the emphasis was upon belief, especially as mediated by the Church, rather than upon people thinking for themselves. There were manuscript books owned by the Church, situated in the monasteries mainly, accessible to few. These were in any case mainly Christian texts, and in Latin. Moreover the Catholic Church did not like people reading the Bible; this activity was considered heretical, and according to the Church the Bible should be read by priests capable of interpreting it correctly. In general the emphasis was upon Christian works, and away from study to do with anything concerning this world, and away from non-Christian thought. Also, education was confined almost exclusively to the clergy or, rather, to some clergy, and was associated with monasteries. It is perhaps fitting that this period of European history has been termed 'the dark ages', although some historians have come to dispute the legitimacy of the term.

However, by the twelfth century, classical authors were being reintroduced into western European culture. This came about through Christian contact with the Islamic empire, where classical authors had been preserved and translated. Pagan scholars from the Roman Empire had gone eastwards with the rise of Christianity, for example to Persia. After the rise of Islam, there was a period in Islamic history that was tolerant of non-Islamic thought, and the latter was actively studied. Baghdad became a centre of learning, as did Toledo. There were Muslim philosophers, such as Averroes in Spain and Avicenna in the Middle East, whose works were then studied in Christian Europe. The main route by which classical and Arabic thought entered Europe was probably through Spain, where there were various people who translated works from Arabic into Latin. However, there were other routes as well. For example, Leonardo Fibonacci of Pisa, the son of a merchant, wrote his Liber Abbaco in 1202 – a book on mathematics, especially algebra. He did this after travelling in Egypt, Syria and Greece and studying under a Muslim teacher. Thus works on mathematics (including from India) entered Europe from the Arab world (8).

The Early Middle Ages transformed into the 'High Middle Ages'. This period was associated with the further revival of the study of classical thought, as well as with the introduction of some ideas and technology from elsewhere in the world. Alongside this new learning, and new technology, some cities began to grow. The new mathematics enabled cathedrals to be built, which became the focus for the new learning. The cathedrals' participants became referred to collectively as *schola* - 'schools', and later as 'universities'. There arose what became known as scholasticism, with classical authors being studied, principally Aristotle. Learning also started to spread to laypeople, not just churchmen. The city of Paris was probably the main centre of intellectual development within Christian Europe at this time (although not the only one), with scholars such as Peter Abelard based there. The scholars of Paris attracted pupils from across Europe. Learning came to be associated with the new cathedrals, in contrast with the monasteries of old.

Importantly, with the growing influence of Aristotle's works, there was a developing belief and confidence that the intellect could be used to study this world, and that what would be discovered thereby would be thoroughly consistent with Christian revelation and belief. Indeed the trivium and quadrivium, which were the non-theological courses of study, came to be seen as important precursors to studying theology itself. The trivium was made up of the study of grammar, logic and rhetoric, and was seen as more elementary. The quadrivium consisted of arithmetic, geometry, astronomy and music. Also, through the High Middle Ages and into the Renaissance, the study of medicine and law became important (9).

The works of Aristotle were central to the new learning. They had begun to be translated into Latin in the twelfth century, and were received with much interest, although also with much concern by the more orthodox. Aristotle's philosophy had emphasised the empirical study of the natural world, and was thus significantly different to both the Christian emphasis upon preoccupation with the next world, and to Plato's emphasis upon the supposedly higher reality of the world of archetypal forms.

There was through the thirteenth century often a reaction against Aristotelian thought, with attempts to suppress it. Nevertheless, the reintroduction of Aristotle has been called 'a turning point in the history of western thought' (10).

Thomas Aquinas, perhaps the main thinker of thirteenth century Europe, was a man who melded Christian and Aristotelian thought, a combination which came to typify scholasticism. Averroes was an important influence upon him – the Spanish philosopher had tried to reconcile classical and general rational thought with the Koran, an attempt which paved the way for Aquinas to attempt something similar with Aristotelian thought and the Bible. Aquinas' teacher had been Albertus Magnus, who had argued the importance of intellectual study of this world, influenced by Aristotle's ideas about science. This led to the first stirrings in Mediaeval Europe of scientific thinking. For example there were Robert Grosseteste and Roger Bacon in England, who began to think along proto-scientific lines. However scholasticism as a whole moved away from actual empirical study of the physical or natural world, and came to be exemplified by argumentation based upon the texts of accepted authors such as Aristotle (11).

The growth of the new learning, with its inclusion of non-Christian thought, must be contrasted with contemporaneous Christian authoritarianism and intolerance. Thus the early thirteenth century saw the beginnings of the Inquisition, to suppress heresy. There was in particular the Albigensian crusade, basically an extremely violent suppression of the 'heretical' Cathars of southern France (12).

However, with the fourteenth century came the further development of western thinking. This was in particular associated with the city states of Italy, although it spread throughout Western Europe. This development, and associated developments in arts and crafts, is what is usually referred to as the Renaissance.

The people of the Italian city states built upon, and took further, the developments of the High Middle Ages. There were in particular the Renaissance 'humanists', scholars who valued classical thought highly. Non-Christian thought became increasingly well-known and respected. Moreover, there developed schools with a new educational curriculum, where young men could study a variety of subjects – including how to run a business and keep accounts (the latter based upon Fibonacci's Liber Abbaco). They also studied classical authors such as Cicero. Literacy, numeracy, business ability, and skill in physical arts and crafts, became much more widespread within the populations of the Italian city states (13).

In the early fourteenth century there came the early Renaissance humanist Petrarch, who was very influential. Indeed it was he who first considered that the previous thousand years had been an age of darkness. Inheriting the revived interest in classical thought, he had however a very different approach to it. Instead of trying to integrate it into Christian thinking, he approached it on its own terms. Although still a devout Christian, he considered that classical thought could be appreciated as the highest form of thinking prior to Christianity. His enthusiasm stimulated an increasing interest in, and revival of, classical thought, which came to be recognised as important in itself, irrespective of whether or not it was consistent with Christianity (14).

Moreover the revival of classical knowledge was associated increasingly with the development of the urban middle class, and with laymen, not just churchmen. Alongside the developments in thinking, and the revival of classical thought, there were inventions stemming from elsewhere in the world which transformed life in the Italian city states, and elsewhere in Europe – in particular there were the magnetic compass, gunpowder, the mechanical clock, paper, and printing (15).

Furthermore, with the decline and fall of Byzantium in the fourteenth and fifteenth centuries, Christian scholars fled west, in particular to the city states in Italy. In consequence ideas from the classical Greek world became increasingly widespread in Western Europe, especially the works of Plato, now accessible in the original

Greek. Platonism offered a different view of the human mind to that of scholastic Aristotelianism. The humanists' Platonism was also different from the more limited use of Plato in earlier Christianity. They had access to the original texts, including those of Plotinus, the Neo-Platonist.

The Platonist and Neo-Platonist philosophies involved belief that the human mind was itself to some extent divine, being the image and likeness of god, and could, through the use of the imagination, come to know god. This approach contrasted with the dry, text-based argumentation into which scholasticism had deteriorated. It also contrasted with orthodox Christian belief that people could only approach god through the church and through the mediation of Christ. Furthermore it was an approach which, through its emphasis upon the importance of the creative imagination, encouraged the development of the arts (16).

There was also a growing interest in the use of mathematics for understanding the world, as in the old Pythagorian philosophy, which was now being studied. This interest of course had also been fed by the influx of mathematical ideas from the non-Christian world. Mathematics came to be applied to understanding the movement of the planets.

The spread of new ideas was further helped by the increasing use of paper on which to write manuscripts. Then, with the invention of moveable type printing in the fifteenth century, those ideas could travel much more quickly. Pamphlets and books became widespread.

Importantly, printing also made available copies of the Bible, translated into local languages, so that people could read it for themselves, independently of the clergy. This helped undermine the power of the Church. Also, the power of the Church had been successfully challenged by secular rulers who disputed its claims to be the prime authority and power. The Catholic Church was also recognised as being very corrupt and in need of reform. Thus the Church was being challenged significantly, as people seriously questioned its teaching and behaviour. From the eleventh and twelfth centuries, and especially under popes such as Innocent III and Gregory VII, the papacy had tried to become the dominant ruler of Europe, to whom local kings were subordinate. This had created a backlash from local rulers, with open warfare at times between them and the papacy. Clerics were also subject only to ecclesiastical law, which often meant that they committed crimes with relative impunity – a further cause of resentment. The local rulers triumphed, especially with the capture of the pope by the French king. The Church came to be seen by many primarily as a corrupt money-making institution.

During the Renaissance, with the rise of printing and the spread of printed books there was one particular classical author who was very widely read. That author was Cicero, a Roman Republican politician who had been a contemporary of Julius Caesar, and who thus lived before the beginnings of Christianity. Cicero was, in his own time, a man who explained Greek philosophical thought to the Romans, and who had written in a very readable and engaging style. He was much influenced by the Stoic philosophers. In particular Cicero was concerned with 'humanitas' (17). This term refers to 'humaneness', or 'humanism', and in particular implies concern for tolerance, consideration of others, and the importance of the liberal arts and education.

Some scholars see the spread of Cicero's works as the key element in the Renaissance. His 'Letters' for example, were a main feature of the education system of the Italian Renaissance. One best-selling Renaissance manuscript book was Leonardo Bruni's work celebrating classical humanism and the arguments and writings of Socrates, Plato and Cicero.

Cicero had written: *"Since the universe is wholly filled with the Eternal Intelligence and the Divine Mind, it must be that human souls are influenced by their contact with divine souls... That animal which we call man, endowed with foresight and quick intelligence, complex, keen, possessing memory, full of reason and prudence, has been given a certain distinguished status by the supreme God who created him..."*

Cicero thus emphasised that 'reason' is what human beings share with the 'Divine Mind'. Furthermore, he wrote: *"There is no single thing so like another, so closely corresponding to it, as are all of us to one another. Consequently to take something away from someone else – to profit by another's loss – is more unnatural than death, or destitution, or pain, or any physical or external blow... Nature's law promotes and coincides with the common interest...."* He also wrote: *"true law is reason, right and natural... Its validity is universal; it is unchangeable and eternal..."* (On the State, III, 22, 33)

Thus Cicero argued the idea that there exists a natural law, a natural morality. This he related to the 'Divine Mind', with 'human souls' being influenced by this Divine Mind, having a spark of divinity to them, in particular the ability to reason (18).

The idea of 'natural law' had probably begun with Aristotle who, in his Rhetoric, stated that: "Particular law is that which each community lays down and applies to its own members: this is partly written and partly unwritten. Universal law is the law of Nature. For there really is, as everyone to some extent divines, a natural justice and injustice that is binding on all men, even on those who have no association or covenant with each other."

The idea of natural law had also been an important element in the teaching of the Stoic philosophers. With the rise of Christianity it fell into disuse as a concept. Augustine in particular considered that living by natural law was not possible since the supposed 'fall' of humanity. However the idea was reintroduced into Catholic Christian thought by Gratian in the twelfth century, and was discussed by Thomas Aquinas in the thirteenth. With the Renaissance the notion of there being a 'natural law', whether moral law or more general, became increasingly influential. This idea then gained added impetus with the rise of science.

Importantly, Cicero's *humanitas* included more than recognition of 'natural law'. It also included the belief that human beings share characteristics related to the 'divine mind', and it emphasised the importance of reason, tolerance and humaneness.

There was one person especially who was much influenced by Cicero. That was the Dutch humanist Erasmus. He was a cleric, and the illegitimate child of a priest, as were many other people at that time in the late fifteenth and early sixteenth centuries. Erasmus lived when printing had not been in existence for very long. He became a bestselling author, of many different books, from a translation of the Greek New Testament to a book on etiquette. It was said at the time: *"with the exception of a few monks and would-be theologians, all learned men are followers of Erasmus"* (Johann Eck 1518).

Erasmus criticised the Catholic Church. He did not see the need for any intermediaries between individual Christians and their scriptures or their god. He emphasised Bible study. He was a pacifist. He was also particularly critical of kings, whom he compared to rapacious eagles. He argued for tolerance and against thinking in terms of 'heresy'. He thought theology should be kept to a minimum, and that people should study the Bible, pray, be ethical and behave well with each other. He considered it of spiritual importance to live a loving and charitable life, rather than to hold to a supposedly correct and actually spiritually irrelevant specific belief.

Erasmus appears to have been a very important influence in the history of Western thought, in various ways (19). In particular, many people were influenced by his arguments for tolerance. However there was increasing pressure to reform the Church, which began to react defensively. More and more people read the Bible for themselves. Then came Martin Luther, and with the rapid spread of his ideas (due to printing) the Reformation began in earnest, as people rebelled against the Catholic Church. Protestantism had begun.

There developed a bitter and violent polarisation between Catholic and Protestant. Whilst many people had wished to follow the teachings of Erasmus, and there was even talk of a 'third church', this did not happen. The arguments of Erasmus for toleration then provoked bitter responses. Religious warfare came to dominate the European world. So, sadly, the toleration preached by Erasmus was superseded by its opposite. Questions of correct belief, and the punishment of supposed heresy, became paramount. There was eventually the Thirty Years War.

Now it was in this context that there came the rise of science, which got underway significantly during the sixteenth and seventeenth centuries, when religious conflict was at its height. There had been precursors of scientific method before the sixteenth century, for example in ancient Greece, in the Islamic world, and further east, especially in China. There had also been proto-scientific ideas in European thought, with people such as Roger Bacon and Robert Grosseteste, associated with the rise of high mediaeval scholasticism and its emphasis on Aristotle. Yet scholasticism had come to prioritise argument and discussion around what was said in accepted books, rather than actual study of the world itself.

One could put it that in the sixteenth century science really began. Personally, I date this beginning to an event in England, during the reign of Elizabeth the First – when William Gilbert studied magnetism. Gilbert carried out a long series of experiments on the properties of magnets. He was, therefore, studying the actual physical world, or specific aspects of it, using experimental method, and not basing his opinions about magnetism on what some accepted scholar said in some text – this latter being the standard practice up until then. Gilbert was critical of this earlier practice, of arguing on the basis of received opinion, instead of empirical study of nature itself (20). Gilbert published a book detailing his experiments and their findings at the end of the sixteenth century. This book was read by the Italian, Galileo Galilei, who devoted his life to scientific experimentation.

At the same time, the philosopher Francis Bacon was also emphasising the study of the world itself, and not following ancient texts, which paralleled Gilbert's message and practice. Bacon argued that knowledge came through a process of 'induction', by which he meant accumulating actual facts about the world and then making generalisations based upon those facts.

Meanwhile Galileo studied various aspects of the physical universe. He studied the motion of objects, as well as gravity. When he came across the recently invented telescope he made an improved version. Using this he could explore the night sky. In doing so he discovered phenomena, for example the moons of Jupiter, whose existence was not previously known, and which contradicted the old opinions about the heavens.

The old Western idea of the universe – that the planets went around the earth, attached to spheres, had already been challenged with Copernicus' theory of the planets being in orbit around the sun. Observations with telescopes supported this idea. The development of mathematics was also helping this process of overturning the old theory about the planets, as mathematics could correctly describe the orbits of the planets. Given that the Church upheld the old idea of the universe, and even that God in his heaven was supposed to exist out beyond the ninth sphere, such new thinking was unsettling. In consequence the Church, at times, resisted the new science. Galileo himself was tried for propounding the Copernican theory. Elsewhere however, within the Protestant Western world especially, the situation was easier for scientists.

Then, in particular, in the latter half of the seventeenth century there came a man whose scientific work was revolutionary. This man was Isaac Newton. He was both an experimenter and a gifted mathematician. He developed the mathematical calculus, and studied optics, gravity and the motion of physical objects. He derived the 'Laws of Motion'. With these, suddenly, human beings could understand physical motion. Newton also studied gravity and derived a mathematical expression for the force of gravity between two bodies. Newton gave humanity a set of intellectual tools for understanding the physical universe, both with regard to the behaviour of objects on earth, and with regard to the motions of planets around the sun. One can describe his work as momentous.

By the time Newton developed his laws of motion, warfare between Christian sects had generally come to a stop, or at least reached a truce. People had learned to tolerate others of somewhat different beliefs, at least if they lived elsewhere. Toleration had actually been developing, partly due to the experience of extended conflict, and partly due to the rise of science. Of course, the idea of toleration had been in existence before, propounded by Erasmus.

By the end of the seventeenth century the concept of toleration began to be taken very seriously once again. For example, the philosopher John Locke wrote his 'Letter Concerning Toleration'. What is interesting in reading this letter is how he argues. He quotes Cicero. Then he quotes the teachings of Jesus and the New Testament, ignoring much in the Bible, for example in the Old Testament, that is the opposite of tolerant. He also explicitly contrasts Christian teaching with the practices of the old Israelites. Locke wrote: *"...but that the church of Christ should persecute others, and force others by fire and sword to embrace her faith and doctrine, I could never yet find in any of the books of the New Testament."* Locke also makes a convincing argument that belief is no concern of the 'magistrate' – in doing so he is providing an escape route, as it were, so that people could let god decide about other people's beliefs and behaviour (21).

Locke also argued on the basis of 'natural law' that people are created equal by god, and have natural rights of life, liberty, health and property. His philosophical writings also display other noteworthy features. He was very much an 'empiricist', and asserted that people learn through experience, through what was termed the 'association of ideas'. This contrasted with belief that human beings possess 'innate ideas' through which they can come to understand the world, and which was a theory which Locke criticised. He also argued that human irrationality stems from the erroneous associations of ideas, and that human moral improvement could be nurtured by the regulation of material conditions.

The works of Newton and Locke were highly influential. There developed what one could call the principles of the Enlightenment, a crucial aspect of eighteenth century Western history. These principles were the importance of using reason based upon evidence, and the importance of toleration. In France, in particular, a group of thinkers emphasised reason. These were the 'philosophes', people such as

D'Alembert and Diderot. In Britain, the emphasis was different, despite the background of Newton and Locke, and was upon the 'social emotions' and there being an innate moral sense. Moral philosophers such as Shaftesbury and Hutcheson emphasised the importance of the social emotions, which were seen as aspects of a natural moral law. These philosophers actually disagreed strongly with Locke's belief that there were no innate ideas, especially so in that they argued for the existence of an innate moral sense.

Importantly, empirical study of the world was justified in terms of there being a god who had created the natural world and who had imbued the natural world with natural laws, which could be discovered empirically. This further strengthened the shift away from reliance on the 'revealed' laws in the Bible. In contrast, the use of reasoning based upon empirical investigation was seen as vital, especially as throughout the eighteenth century, scientific discoveries were increasing. There was also a growing sense of optimism, with the belief that god had been 'providential', and had arranged the world for human benefit.

The study of nature, in various areas, came to be taken very seriously. The model for this was the development in knowledge of physics, and Newton's laws of motion. These were understood as god's laws in the physical world. The idea of 'natural law' with respect to morality also gained ground. Thus it was believed that God had created human beings and that there is a natural ethical dimension to life. As I have discussed, Christianity had not stressed the idea of natural law; it had stressed revelation, although the idea of natural law had not been absent from Christian thought. The classical idea came to the fore by the eighteenth century. It was believed that God had created the universe with its natural laws, and that we can find out those laws, such as Newton's laws of motion, or the laws of morality. It also came to be believed that we can study human society and find out what natural laws there are in society, as well as the natural laws pertaining to the human mind and human behaviour – that we can study ourselves, our actions, and our own minds, and thereby discover god's natural laws.

It is important to reflect upon the development of this belief that there are natural laws. This is associated with the rise of science, especially physical science, but it has a particularly theistic interpretation to it, as the 'laws' are believed to have been set by God. This interpretation is however different from the emphasis of traditional Christianity, on revelation. Hence the theism of the Enlightenment age was what one could call a 'natural law' theism, and was influenced by classical thought, and also influenced by the development of science, and it was moving away from traditional Catholic Christianity.

Indeed, people began to question Christianity more and more. Some became deists, people who believed in a god, but who no longer took Christian dogma seriously. The deists' conception of god was a benevolent one. By the early eighteenth century there were also atheists, particularly amongst the French philosophes. It was possible to declare oneself an atheist without being persecuted (at least for some people in some places).

Furthermore, as science progressed, with ever new discoveries, this gave increasing support to the idea that the use of empirically based reasoning was vital to understanding anything. This dynamic very much undermined the old belief that understanding came from the study of accepted texts by authorities such as Aristotle. It would also eventually undermine many people's belief in the Bible. Moreover, as science progressed so technology developed apace, transforming much in the Western world. This included agriculture, with the result that a larger population could be fed. The invention of machines revolutionised both agriculture and the manufacture of other articles, such as clothing. The population increased. Through these changes society changed greatly. Thus science is revolutionary – people discover new aspects of the world, and develop better understanding of the world. This allows them to make old articles better, and to make completely new ones. That technological change is then revolutionary in its turn, transforming human culture and society, for better or worse.

By the nineteenth century the physical sciences were making major progress. People in the nineteenth century were still in the main theists, although atheism was growing in popularity. However people were thinking increasingly in terms of physical science. They applied such thinking to the human world – in other words they were thinking about the human world in similar ways to how they thought about the physical world. They believed that similar natural laws applied to both. I will call this belief 'physicalism'. An influential example of physicalism was the philosophy of Herbert Spencer, which I shall be discussing in chapters four and five.

So by the nineteenth century the development of ideas was very much influenced by the physical sciences. At the same time, Christianity had undergone major changes. It had split from being one church (in Western Europe) into a multitude of different churches. I would also argue that there had come about a change of emphasis amongst its doctrines, a change of emphasis towards the teachings of Jesus, and towards toleration, and away from the Old Testament's violent god, as well as a changed emphasis onto the concept of god-given 'natural laws' and away from 'revelation'. These developments had occurred under the influence of classical thought, and one could put it that the western world had reclaimed its classical heritage. In doing so it had tamed the authoritarian nature of Christianity, developed the physical sciences, and rediscovered the idea of there being a natural morality – a morality associated with humaneness and the 'social emotions'.

3

The Positive Western Tradition

In the last chapter I looked at certain aspects of the development of western thought which I consider the most important, overall, for understanding that general development. I will argue in this and the next chapter that there have been both positive and negative sides to the history of western thought, both of which have had major historical consequences. Related to this, as a Buddhist and psychologist, I am also aware that the ideas people hold affect them significantly, strongly influencing what they do, what effects they have on the world around them, and also the mental states they have. These consequences can also be positive or negative.

Here I will look at some of the very important positives, then turn to some of the negatives in the next chapter. In part, I am here rejoicing in the merits of Western ideas, and of the people who had them, as well as the behaviour that went with them. In doing this I am also fully aware that there have been negative ideas, with very negative effects. But I do very much want to acknowledge and celebrate the positives. I am also aware that personally I have been very fortunate, being born at a time, and in a place, so that I grew up benefitting from the effects of these positive ideas and associated practices. I would like that benefit, shared by others of my generation, to be passed on to as many people as possible, now and in the future.

In my first chapter I took us back to our hunter gatherer ancestors. I mentioned that those hunter gatherers were an intelligent animal species, who could cooperate with each other but who were also a violent species. I explored why they were violent, by focusing upon a crucial issue for hunter gatherers, which I termed the 'fundamental dilemma'. I stressed the violence, and that it is part of our nature. I asked the question: could that hunter gatherer species ever learn to overcome their violence, and ever feed themselves, and feel secure without resorting to violence? Could that ever happen?

Now in this context it is interesting, if we come forward thousands of years, to the time of the Buddha himself, and if we look at the texts where the Buddha is talking about his own life, especially his own 'going forth' into the life of a homeless religious wanderer, and the specific reasons he went forth (the reasons he gave, not later legends about it). It is very interesting that one thing that the Buddha emphasised was that it was human beings being violent to each other that was an important reason for his renunciation – he saw that human life can be deeply unsatisfactory, and that violence was an important aspect of that. He then taught non-violence and non-hatred. He also exemplified these qualities in his life and teaching.

There is an incident in the Buddha's life when he walked between two opposing tribal armies – he was related to those on each side. There was a drought, and an argument had started about who should have the water. He walked between them and asked them some questions: first, what were they going into battle about? Initially they could not tell him, but it gradually emerged that the battle was about water. So the Buddha then asked them how much some drops of water are worth. They replied 'very little'. Then he asked them how much the life of a warrior was worth. They replied 'beyond price'. He then told them 'it is not right that what is beyond price should be spent on what is worth very little.' (1)

They did not fight. Personally, I find that a very moving example of how the Buddha could influence people positively, in a very difficult situation, and how he himself embodied non-violence and non-hatred. Of course, sadly in many circumstances such an approach is unlikely to work, although it illustrates that if there is someone both sides respect then having them as a mediator can at times be very helpful and effective.

However, the Buddha did not just teach that we should abstain from violence and overcome our hatred. He taught that we should actively cultivate and practise love and compassion – *metta* and *karuna*. He also taught people *how* to do that.

In the old Buddhist texts there is one depicting the Buddha's description of the practice of the '*metta bhavana*' – the meditation to develop love and kindness. There is something very striking about what he said in this. The Buddha talked about developing *metta*, developing love, towards all beings – and he compared it to the love of a mother for her child (2). I consider this very significant.

First of all, it is very significant because, not only were those hunter gatherers intelligent, cooperative and violent, but they were also creatures of attachment. *We* are creatures of attachment. By 'attachment' I mean something very positive – we are creatures who have close, warm relationships with each other, typically beginning with a mother's love for her child. Such attachments are integral to being human.

It is also not just that we are mammals and that human maternal love is, at least in part, a mammalian trait. In human beings maternal care is more important still. We are born so immature. A mother's care is vital to us. Furthermore, one thing that I have learned over the years, as a psychologist and as a Buddhist, is the importance of childhood attachments and their effects later on in life – and how central this issue is for human beings. So I find it very interesting that what the Buddha focused upon was something intrinsically human and also vital to our well-being. However there is a further point. Love is not just intrinsically human, not only vital for ordinary human life, but the cultivation of love is the basis for, is central to, spiritual life, to the development of Enlightenment.

Now if we consider maternal love, what aspects does it have? Well, firstly, there is a delight in the child. Then there is also a very warm concern for the wellbeing of the child, not just emotionally but through behaving sensitively toward the child, and actively providing for their needs, so that the child can grow healthily as a human being and eventually develop independence from the mother, becoming an adult. Maternal love has those different aspects.

So it is of crucial significance that the Buddha, in his description of the *metta bhavana* meditation, was telling us to develop love, for everyone, for every living thing, love very much akin to a mother's love for her child. The Buddha was not just teaching non-violence, non-hatred. He was teaching the cultivation of love, and of the development of sensitive loving, caring relationships with other human beings.

Now the question is - those hunter gatherers, with those attributes, how have they, how have *we*, done? How much have we overcome the negatives, and how much have we moved towards expressing the positives, to expressing such love? How much have we been able to succeed in overcoming the limitations of our hunter gatherer species? In particular, how have we done in the West? In the West in the last two thousand years or so? How well have we succeeded in being non-violent and overcoming hatred, and in developing what one could call a 'maternal care' for other people?

In thinking about this I have been considering my own experience, and the circumstances in which I grew up. I was born in the East End of London, in the nineteen fifties. I have various strong memories of being a four or five year old, and of the environment I was in.

I come from a working class family. I was born in a street which like many others had the 'debris' (pronounced in Cockney 'debbry'). A debris was a patch of waste land with various heaps of old bricks overgrown with weeds and convolvulus. There were lots of debris around. There was the debris at one end of the street, and another at the other end. There was also one just over the garden fence, and others in nearby roads. As I learned, a debris was where bombs had fallen during the Second World War. I was born eight years after that war had ended. Its effects were still very much in evidence. I also learned from my relatives about the war. My father and uncles had all fought in it. Then I did not think more about it. Later I learned about World War One, and about other wars in Europe and elsewhere.

The interesting issue I find, looking back, is that I have had no personal experience of war. I used to think 'well, that's the way it is'. It seemed to me for a long time that that was the nature of things, that is, not experiencing war. But actually that is not the case.

Nations in Western Europe have not been to war with each other for nearly seventy years. If one compares that with what happened in Europe over the centuries before, it is an extraordinary change. If one looks at liberal democracies in the world over this period, the same is true. It has been commented upon very strongly that the state of mind of people in liberal democracies, towards each other, has changed. Once upon a time people used to consider that war was natural. But now it is almost inconceivable that liberal democracies would go to war with each other. This is taken for granted. But it is not something we should take for granted. It is actually quite remarkable.

I used to think there was lots of violence around, for example World War Two. I never gained the impression that human violence was on the decline. But it is intriguing that if one studies western democracies with regard to violence, especially the expression of violence, then it is remarkable that human violence has declined. Of course, there are still exceptions to this general rule, for example for people in many inner cities there has been an increase, to some extent, in violent crime. But, when one looks at various statistics about it, the general conclusion to be drawn is that there has been, over the centuries, a decline in violence.

Extraordinarily, even if one includes the two world wars in ones statistics, it is still the case that the average human being in a Western democracy is less likely to experience violence, to be killed in war, or to be murdered. Violence has declined, *per member of population*, to an extraordinary degree since a couple of thousand years ago. We do not actually realise this. I emphasise the 'per member of population', as the large rise in human population can obscure this issue. Moreover the media focus upon reporting violence. In contrast, what history books typically do not indicate is just how much violence there has been, including just how many wars and conflicts there were in the past. For example consider the statistics concerning murder. In the thirteenth century in Western Europe the murder rate was a hundred times what it is now. If one takes almost any measure of violence, it has dropped since those times. Moreover, even in mediaeval times it was much lower than in hunter gatherer times. Of course, there are still areas in which violence is far too common; I could single out bullying amongst children and teenagers as an example of this, and especially inner-city teenage gang violence.

Nevertheless it is actually very interesting that human beings, though we still have a long way to go, have somehow managed, by whatever means, to be less violent than we were. Moreover, if one studies European social history and looks at how people behaved in, for example, 1300 to 1400, one gains the impression that people had less self-control then, and as well as being more violent, were generally much less 'civilised'. I mentioned in my second chapter that Erasmus had authored a book on etiquette. It had been needed.

So somehow, over the centuries, we have become less violent (3). Therefore it is interesting, thinking back to the Buddha and Buddhist precepts of non-hatred and non-violence, that somehow the human race, or at least parts of it, have been able to implicitly put those precepts of non-violence into effect, more successfully than people used to, and over the last sixty years far more than before. It is remarkable, but we have managed this.

I mentioned coming from a working class family in East London. My parents left school aged fourteen. They had to go to work, as their families needed the money. So they could not continue with their education, whereas I went to school until eighteen, and then to university. I had a grant for the latter. Thus I had a free education, not just at school but at university.

Then consider poverty. My parents used to describe to me the poverty there had been in the streets nearby before the Second World War. I have personally never known poverty. I grew up with the 'welfare state'. I also grew up with what one could describe as the 'good, old fashioned' National Health Service. So in these ways I have been very fortunate.

If we go back to the Buddha talking about cultivating love, it is not just that somehow in Western Europe we have been able to implicitly follow the precept of non-violence more successfully, it is also that the love the Buddha talked about has been expressed on a social level – that to some degree, in terms of people actually caring for each other, that became institutionalised – with the provision of free health care, and free education. I find that very interesting. What I would like to rejoice in is that human beings have come a long way, and that we can actually do these things.

Of course, now, fifty or sixty years on from immediate post-war Britain, things are not so easy. I can far too readily bring to mind various serious problems with the provision of health care and education (problems that stem in part from the negative ideas I shall be discussing). But I want to rejoice in my parents' generation, who contributed to that rise in general care for others.

Moreover, I also grew up in a period of rising prosperity. When I was four Harold Macmillan, the Prime Minister, told people they had 'never had it so good'. He was quite correct. This was true not just in Britain or Western Europe. There were wider factors responsible for the growth of well-being, in Western Europe and elsewhere. There was the Marshall Plan of economic aid aimed at stimulating the economies of the nations who received it. It is of note that this was given to defeated nations, Germany and Japan. This was completely different to the end of World War One, when money was taken from the defeated - with disastrous effects. After the Second World War, people had learned their lesson – having defeated your enemy you do not 'do them down'.

That is itself interesting and well worth celebrating. But also, between the end of World War Two and my birth, something else happened. This was the publication of the United Nations Declaration of Human Rights. This was due in no small part to Eleanor Roosevelt, who chaired the committee that brought it about, and who therefore has become a heroine of mine. I am going to quote some excerpts from it:

"All human beings are born free and equal in dignity and rights. They are endowed with reason and conscience and should act towards one another in a spirit of brotherhood.

Everyone is entitled to all the rights and freedoms set forth in this Declaration, without distinction of any kind, such as race, colour, sex, language, religion, political or other opinion, national or social origin, property, birth or other status."

It then goes on for some thirty articles, spelling out specific rights (4). Many of these articles are about people's rights not to be on the receiving end of violence, and not to be on the receiving end of the arbitrary and harmful use of power. Others of the articles are about people's rights to education, rights to health care, and so forth.

Again, I find this very interesting. This is a document on a political level that actually spells out what are underlying moral precepts. It spells them out in a legislative form as 'rights'. But it is really encouraging the enactment of specific moral principles, such as non-violence, as well as making explicit the circumstances through which human beings flourish psychologically and spiritually. Moreover it states that people 'should act towards one another in a spirit of brotherhood', and there is also an article mentioning ones duty to the community. Personally, I find it a remarkable document, and remarkable that human beings could produce it.

Of course, over the years it has been criticised. Moreover, the doctrine of human rights – natural rights - has come under criticism. Actually in the eighteenth century the philosopher Jeremy Bentham described the idea of natural human rights as 'nonsense on stilts'. The thinking underlying his criticism is that rights come from governments, from human beings. So how can one have underlying 'natural' rights – it does not make sense. (Bentham was an atheist.) There has been much philosophical debate about that over the years. There have been other objections as well. Indeed there have been countries that did not want to uphold these rights. The countries that, in the first place, did not sign the UN Declaration were the Soviet Union and some of its European communist puppet states, South Africa, and Saudi Arabia. Of course, if you are a totalitarian or very authoritarian regime then you will inevitably be opposed to the very idea of natural human rights.

More recently there has been much debate about whether the idea of human rights has been used more than it should, or even been misused. I think that there is truth in such criticisms. In answer I will read a quote from the philosopher A.C. Grayling. He is discussing scepticism about human rights, and how this could be rebutted:

"But in fact the chief rebuttal comes from the history... of how the rights were claimed and won with so much struggle. A mature, reflective exercise of gathering the hard-won lessons and even harder-won advances of five centuries into a single document distilling that experience is itself an achievement of the human spirit that dwarfs the nay-sayers, motivated as they seem to be by a lack of understanding of what it would be like to stand on the kindling at the stake as the fire is lit under you, as inquisitors practise the water torture on you, as you languish in prison for your beliefs, as you slave in the fields or go hungry and in rags to the factory before dawn, as you live a life on the margin of society excluded from the goods and possibilities available to the mainstream, as the midnight knock comes at the door, as your children are torn from you and marched towards the gas chamber. In the absence of direct experience of hardship, suffering and exclusion, enslavement and discrimination, persecution and murder, the next resource is moral imagination. The ground of scepticism too often lies in its lack." (5)

I consider this a very strong plea for the importance of the concept of human rights. If one considers this concept to be problematic or erroneous, then one has to consider what happens when it is implicitly or explicitly denied.

I also consider it somewhat ironic that Grayling can give that defence, as I am aware that he is an atheist. If one reads his book about the development of human rights it is quite interesting how he describes this development. He begins with the struggle for religious liberty, and the overcoming of the intolerance and authoritarianism of Christianity up to and including the Reformation.

I find this interesting, as the doctrine of human rights developed very much in the context of Christianity, albeit a changing Christianity. Of course, Grayling's discussion of old violations of human rights in Christianity is correct – for a long time Christianity did not recognise what we now call human rights; it did not tolerate non-believers. Even after the Reformation, and especially at that time, if people did not believe what you believed, they were killed. It seemed right to do this. But I will give another quote, from another Declaration. This is from the United States Declaration of Independence:

"We hold these truths to be self-evident; that all men are created equal; that they are endowed by their Creator with certain unalienable rights; that among these are life, liberty, and the pursuit of happiness; that to secure these rights governments are instituted among men, deriving their just powers from the consent of the governed..."

If one compares the words of the two Declarations they are remarkably similar. But one thing has been removed in the United Nations Declaration – God.

Thus in the context of the world as whole, with its varieties of belief systems, the concept of God has been explicitly dropped. Yet the thinking behind the UN Declaration, thinking which is explicit in the United States Declaration of Independence, is very clearly related to the concept of God – with the ideas that all human beings are created equal, and endowed by their creator with certain rights. God is seen as the law giver; and he gives natural rights to all human beings. Indeed the United States Declaration explicitly mentions "the laws of nature and of nature's God".

Now an important question arises: if that is where the idea of human rights specifically comes from, if one were to drop the idea of God, what is one left with, as a basis for believing in the existence of those rights?

In asking that question I am very aware that the concept of human rights has been taken very seriously over the last sixty years, but that if one looks at moral philosophy what is evident is that if one leaves out the idea of God then one is left in a very difficult place, if one is not a Buddhist. Over the last sixty years or so what has grown up in moral philosophy is the doctrine of 'relativism' – that morality is something decided by particular groups, particular cultures; that there is no naturally existing morality.

So there is an interesting juxtaposition, with on the one hand the rise of moral relativism, and on the other human rights being taken increasingly seriously. There is thus a very noteworthy dichotomy between a common political acceptance of the existence of natural human rights alongside a lack of any moral philosophy on which to base them – unless one believes in God or is a Buddhist.

As a Buddhist I would emphasise that that there *is* a natural morality, which is not dependent upon a God legislating. I recognise morality as an inherent aspect of human existence, as I discussed in my first chapter, which relates ultimately to the fact that each of us is not a separate, inherently existent self.

Now if we look at the development of the concept of human rights over the centuries, then this development has been associated with that of other ideas and the practices based upon them – those ideas being liberty, equality, democracy, the individual, toleration, and the use of reason based upon evidence.

These ideas seem to go together, and to have developed alongside each other. For example, various of them are mentioned in both Declarations to which I have referred. These ideas were developed from the time of the Renaissance. That development was however particularly associated with the eighteenth century and the age of Enlightenment. It was also associated, although not exclusively so, with the political movement that came to be called Liberalism. Indeed, these ideas are central aspects of liberal democracies.

Actually, if one studies the history of Liberalism one realises that these ideas, although expressed in words, were not necessarily put into practice (6). It is easier to say these things than to enact them. Moreover, terms such as 'liberty' are easy to use when referring to oneself and one's own needs. It is not so easy to apply them to other people. For example, if one considers the United States Declaration of Independence, and its statement 'all men are created equal', there is a huge irony. At the time of that Declaration parts of the United States were slave owning. There is also the issue of how people in the United States treated native Americans. These are of course serious contradictions with the meanings of the words used in the Declaration. In fact, the move towards acting upon those ideas took a lot longer than the expression of them in words in a document. People can of course be self-contradictory, people such as the Founding Fathers of the United States and their supporters. However, a phrase such as 'all men are created equal' can escape any one person's own particular use of it. It can be taken up by other people. It is a phrase that has a life of its own.

So the actual development of rights came more slowly. Moreover, in particular, women at first got missed out. It took quite a while for the penny to drop - 'all' means all – everybody, not just oneself. It actually applies to everyone. But if one studies the last sixty years one sees the development of actual human rights in various ways, for example the rights of gay people not to be imprisoned or persecuted. Overall, rights came slowly, and there is also still a way to go. In some parts of the world there is a very, very long way to go. But I celebrate the improvement in human rights that there has been.

I mentioned the irony of the United States Declaration of Independence, with the United States being a slave owning country. It is interesting to look back at the abolition of the slave trade, and how this spread across the world in the late eighteenth and early nineteenth centuries. I will quote Rowan Williams on this:

"Apart from Christianity, what were or what could have been the factors that could drive any critique of slavery in the eighteenth century? We think of the Age of Enlightenment as an intellectual climate in which the assumptions of modern liberal and democratic thought were first formed; and that is not wholly wrong. But you will look in vain to the secularising writers of the period for systematic

criticisms of slavery, let alone campaigns for its ending. The liberal and egalitarian principles of the French Enlightenment made not the slightest dent upon the slave system (and the post-Revolution French administrations made no move towards emancipation of their own accord)" (7)

With regard to Britain, I find it very interesting that the slave trade was abolished (and eventually slavery deemed illegal) mainly due to the efforts of a group of evangelical Christians, spearheaded by William Wilberforce. I also find this remarkable, because Britain's prosperity had grown due to the slave trade, and was still very much dependent upon it.

The West African slave trade had existed before Europeans, and before Britons, ever got involved with it. There was both active West African involvement in it, as well as Muslim. But Britain became very involved in the trade, and with the exploitation of it to provide labour in the Caribbean and America. It is truly remarkable how relatively quickly, due to the influence of the evangelicals and Wilberforce, Britain banned the slave trade. It even sent part of the Royal Navy to combat the slave trade. Moreover the ban on the slave trade would have happened more quickly if the Napoleonic wars had not intervened as they slowed up the process of abolition. People were quite rapidly persuaded that it was not acceptable – that slavery is completely out of the question, completely inhuman.

Slavery had of course existed for millenia. The first recorded attempt at the abolition of slavery was that by the Indian emperor Ashoka, over two thousand years ago. Ashoka started off like other violent warlords, but he converted to Buddhism, and felt remorse for his past violence. One aspect of the expression of his remorse was an attempt to ban slavery.

However, in Britain in recent centuries, abolition was very much to do with Christian evangelicals. It seems, looking at the evangelicals, that what was important for them was taking the principles, the teachings, of Jesus, and acting upon them. Also, they recognised very much that if one harms someone else one is also harming oneself. They recognised that participating in a society that allows the slave trade to happen is simply out of the question. They recognised that it is one's duty, one's responsibility, to act to abolish such an institution.

This is very interesting, and very much worth celebrating – that Christian morality contains a teaching on love (which is what the Evangelicals were focusing upon, and not the teachings of the Old Testament), and that this was acted upon.

In general, in looking at the development of rights, as well as those other ideas, I see those ideas developing in an interplay between Christian thought and classical thought, especially ideas such as those expressed by Cicero that I quoted in my second chapter, concerning 'humanitas'. There was also the influence of scientific thought. Each type of thinking could influence the others, and this mutual influence had some very positive aspects to it, including the development of ideas such as tolerance and human rights. The historical details of this development are complex, with many different religious and political groups involved. However there was in particular the influence of the British moral philosophers of the eighteenth century, who tend not to be acknowledged, although their emphasis upon the existence of a natural moral sense, associated with the 'social emotions', was very important (8). Indeed Britain in the eighteenth century saw the development of many moral and philanthropic movements and institutions – such as 'Friendly Societies', and Methodism (with its emphasis upon education and helping people). The evangelicals' stance against slavery was part of this overall movement.

From a Buddhist point of view ideas such as 'liberty' are well worth exploring. If we explore the implications of the term 'liberty' for example - liberty is freedom for the individual to think what one believes to be true, and not what one is told to think. As a Buddhist I very much appreciate living in a society where I can do that. Such a society stands in stark contrast to the theistic one in which unbelievers have few or no rights, or unbelief is punishable with death.

Moreover, in looking at the idea of liberty, this reminds me of the Buddha's words - that his teaching has 'one taste, the taste of freedom'. That freedom is a radical spiritual freedom, but a very important point to realise with this is that the opportunity to develop radical spiritual freedom is dependent upon social and political conditions. They have to be able to support the liberty of the individual to think and act upon how their conscience and reason takes them. There is thus a very important link between liberty of conscience and thought, and the ability to develop the psychological and spiritual freedom recognised by the Buddha.

Then there is the concept of the 'individual', a concept developed to contrast with the idea that we are each just a part of a social order, a social group. The development of the concept of the individual allows people to get away from the dictates of the group and its leaders. It is a very interesting concept - 'the individual'. I am reminded of Sangharakshita's teaching about the 'Individual' (9). He contrasted the 'Individual' (or 'true individual') on the one hand with a person who just fits into a group, and on the other hand with the 'individualist', who does what they want without reference to others. It is a central aspect of spiritual practice, that we each develop autonomy, and become 'true individuals', but not individualists – in other words that we become autonomous individuals in relationship to each other, and to other people. Human beings are creatures of relationships. It is part of our nature. The question is not about ignoring or forgetting about relationships, but about developing the quality and nature of those relationships.

I stress the importance of this, because I am aware that in Western thought, particularly in Liberalism, thinking about the idea of the individual can be problematic. On the one hand, the emphasis on the concept of the 'individual' is a very important aspect of the Liberal tradition, especially the consideration that each individual is important and should have the liberty to think and act according to their conscience. On the other hand, I get the strong impression, in studying Liberal thought, that the individual is considered to exist almost as if in a social vacuum, with society and the complex networks of human relationships being considered very secondary, even fictions (10). This is the polar opposite of other political (or religious) ideologies that rigidly subordinate the individual to society, where the individual is considered to matter very little in themselves and forced to comply with whatever beliefs are imposed upon them by society, as if the latter is more real.

So as a Buddhist I am aware of the importance of individuality, and that being an individual involves being autonomous, but that this autonomy is always in relationship with other people. We are intrinsically creatures of relationship, although at times, sometimes completely and irrevocably, we also have to go forth from the rules and beliefs of the groups to which we belong, to be faithful to the truth and to the duties of natural morality.

One could also take those other positive western ideas that I mentioned and compare them with specifically Buddhist principles. For example one could look at the use of 'reason based upon evidence' and how the Buddha described that very practice in his discourses (11). However, coming back to the crucial idea of human rights, what I have been aware of is its development in a Christian context, as a legalistic idea, with god as the natural legislator. In more recent years, in contrast, there has been the development of moral relativism, the belief that morals are just a matter of cultural choice and opinion. I am very aware of, and concerned about, that disparity and its influence. This is an issue to which I will return in a later chapter.

In general, I celebrate the positive ideas from the Western tradition, the idea of human rights, and the ideas that go with it, as well as the behaviour that has been associated with them. However I am concerned that these days the foundations on which they are built are crumbling. Moreover, in the political world, across the political spectrum, the superstructure of political activity has become separated from those foundations. In part this is due to the continuing influence of negative ideas from the western tradition, some of which I look at in my next essay. I think it is very important that the underpinnings of the positive ideas, especially the underpinning that is natural morality, become understood more generally. Otherwise, firstly, political thought will stay on the level of polarised but superficial debate, and be in effect little more than the modern equivalent of tribal conflict; and, secondly, what has been gained could well be lost. I am very concerned that the positives are kept and strengthened. So I rejoice in the positives of western thought. I hope they continue to be influential for a very long time. Moreover I consider that Buddhists in particular need to actively and constructively help with that continuation.

4

Harmful Developments in Western Thought

In the preceding chapters I explored the idea of 'natural law'. This is a term which has been applied specifically in the concept of natural moral law, but also generally in the idea that there exist natural laws in the world, for example the laws of physics but also supposedly similar natural laws underlying human behaviour and human society.

In my third chapter I explored some positive developments that came out of this background, concepts such as 'human rights'. I also looked at behaviour associated with this, such as the decline in levels of violence in the western world, a development some people find surprising. In this chapter I will explore some negative developments. I will investigate some ideas that arose that have had major negative impacts on the world. I will look, from a Buddhist point of view, at how those ideas can be expressions of, and encourage, craving, hatred and delusion. I will also argue that these negative developments stem from the misapplication of ideas, from nineteenth century physical and biological science, to the human world. This misapplication was bound up with the belief that there exist similar natural laws underlying human behaviour to those governing classical physics.

In particular, in this chapter I will be exploring three sets of ideas: neoclassical economics, 'social evolutionism', and Marxism. I have chosen ideas that go across the political spectrum. These ideas developed in the eighteenth and, particularly, the nineteenth, centuries. They have had lasting effects into the twenty-first century.

I will begin with a quote. This is from the New York Times, in 2009. It is written by a leading economist, Paul Krugman (1).

"It's hard to believe now, but not long ago economists were congratulating themselves over the success of their field. Those successes — or so they believed — were both theoretical and practical,

leading to a golden era for the profession... Last year, everything came apart. Few economists saw our current crisis coming, but this predictive failure was the least of the field's problems. More important was the profession's blindness to the very possibility of catastrophic failures in a market economy. During the golden years, financial economists came to believe that markets were inherently stable — indeed, that stocks and other assets were always priced just right. There was nothing in the prevailing models suggesting the possibility of the kind of collapse that happened last year."

So why did economists consider that such a crisis was not a possibility? How did they get in that position? To begin to answer that, let us go back to the eighteenth century, to the age of the Enlightenment.

At that time people were beginning to hold an optimistic view of human beings, and of nature and the world. This was due, at least in part, to the fact that the human world around them was beginning to change, and change for the better. There had been major developments in mathematics and physics, especially Newton's laws of motion, discovered in the previous century. There had been philosophers such as John Locke, emphasising tolerance and using reason based upon experience. Newton and Locke had a tremendous influence throughout the European world. People were beginning to have much more positive ideas about what human beings could do. They were beginning to take seriously the idea there could be progress. They were also taking seriously the idea that God had created the natural world for us, and that he had created a world which is positive.

They also developed a more positive idea of human beings that contrasted with the earlier Christian emphasis on humans as sinners. Indeed, people thought that even the faults of human beings could actually work out for the benefit of all. Some quotations from the eighteenth century writer Alexander Pope give the flavour of this optimism:

"Thus God and Nature linked the general frame, And bade Self-love and Social be the same."

"...the balance of happiness among Mankind is kept even by Providence"

"God intends happiness to be equal"

So there was a sense that the world and human beings are essentially positive, and that this is intended and brought about by God (2). With the rise and development of physical science, and with the associated inventions and developing technology, the world was certainly changing, and demonstrating what empirically based reasoning could do. As the eighteenth century went on, change got ever faster. Many people were coming to be very optimistic, and they had a sense that the human world could develop for the better, that it could evolve.

Such ideas passed into early thinking about the economic world. People got the impression that the developing world of trade and commerce was a positive force, and that even if someone acted selfishly, in their own interest, in selling or buying something, that nevertheless that could contribute to everybody's welfare. For example, Adam Smith wrote:

"By preferring the support of domestic to that of foreign industry, he intends only his own security; and by directing that industry in such a manner as its produce may be of the greatest value, he intends only his own gain, and he is in this, as in many other cases, led by an invisible hand to promote an end which was no part of his intention. Nor is it always the worse for the society that it was not part of it. By pursuing his own interest he frequently promotes that of the society more effectually than when he really intends to promote it."

Adam Smith was stating that people can engage in trade for their own benefit, but that actually that can benefit other people (3). He used the phrase 'an invisible hand'. Now this is another phrase that has taken on a life of its own. It came to mean the 'invisible hand' of the market. But of course in the eighteenth century the 'invisible hand' could also mean God's hand. People believed God is 'providential', making things positive for people - so that, even if someone is being selfish, the invisible hand, either of the market or God, can make their actions work in the general interest.

Thus people were looking at trade, looking at commerce, as something that could be inherently beneficial. There is sense in this. Trade between two groups can be beneficial to both sides, whilst war can harm both, and tends to have only one side 'winning'. People even saw commerce as something that might sweep away the old warfare, through nations developing trading links with each other that were of mutual benefit. It would therefore be foolish for them to go to war, as both would lose. (Associated with the positive emphasis on trade and commerce there was also, of course, the political aspirations of the rising middle classes, and an implicit contrast with the aristocracy.)

At the same time there were other developments in ideas. Some people were deliberately thinking in non-theistic terms. A new form of moral theory was growing up, called utilitarianism. This was first developed by Jeremy Bentham. It was based around a concept called 'utility'. He did not coin the term; it had been used by David Hume and Hugo Grotius. Bentham defined 'utility' as follows:

"By utility is meant that property in any object, whereby it tends to produce benefit, advantage, pleasure, good, or happiness, (all this in the present case comes to the same thing) or (what comes again to the same thing) to prevent the happening of mischief, pain, evil, or unhappiness to the party whose interest is considered: if that party be the community in general, then the happiness of the community: if a particular individual, then the happiness of that individual." (4)

Utilitarianism is an atheistic moral theory, although it does have roots in Christianity. (Augustine had used the Latin term 'utile' to refer to what was morally good, but supposedly secondary in importance to loving God.). Utilitarians saw what is moral as that which increases utility for anybody. Also, if the utility of the community as a whole is increased in some way, then that is seen as morally good. If utility is decreased then that is seen as morally bad.

Now utility is not a very clear concept. In fact it is very confused. Bentham described utility as a property 'in' an object, but he is actually referring to various different things - the influences of that object, the uses of that object, the psychological benefits of that object, sometimes its material benefits. These are not properties 'in' the object itself. Often they are psychological responses to the object. Moreover the same object may be used by different people with different degrees of benefit to them – a bowl of porridge is likely to be of much greater value to a starving man than to a millionaire. Its value, its 'utility', is not a property of the object by itself. Furthermore, how can one state that different benefits are in any way of equal utility? It seems to make little sense to compare the supposed utility of a piece of music with the supposed utility of eating necessary food. In general 'utility' is a confused and poorly defined concept.

Then Bentham is saying that what is morally good is whatever increases utility. From a Buddhist perspective there is something very wrong with this. It is completely ignoring the motivation behind an action. It is just going to the effects, or supposed effects, of an action. In fact Bentham was very critical of the idea of thinking in terms of motivation. So if I use the term 'craving', and state that someone is motivated by craving, Bentham would have dismissed that as nonsense.

From a Buddhist perspective the concept of utility can easily be seen to rationalise immoral behaviour or motivation. Somebody could be increasing their utility, in other words getting pleasure out of something, but actually they are getting pleasure whilst motivated by craving or hatred. So from a Buddhist perspective the concept is very problematic.

Despite its serious limitations, during the nineteenth century utilitarianism developed into one of the dominant forms of moral philosophy, becoming increasingly influential. Its influence grew at the same time that science was developing. Physical science was developing rapidly, and having major effects on the world. Newton's laws of motion were being applied to a whole variety of different areas.

In the nineteenth century this included thermodynamics – the properties, in particular the energy, of collections of atoms. People were becoming very impressed by physical science, that is by Newtonian science, and becoming very interested in the application of the methods of physical science to the human world. The belief was that God had made the material cosmos, Newton had discovered natural laws to the physical world, and one could apply such ideas to the human world, and discover similar laws there. Such thinking became highly influential as the nineteenth century unfolded.

This use of ideas, from the physical sciences, in the human world has sometimes been called 'scientism'. I prefer to use the term 'physicalism', which emphasises its fundamental characteristic. (The older term also has the possible implication that 'science' necessarily involves thinking in physical terms, a belief with which I disagree.)

So by the middle of that century people were thinking extremely seriously in terms of understanding the human world in very physical terms. For example, there was the philosopher Herbert Spencer, whom I mentioned briefly before. He was world famous, and very influential in Europe, in the USA, and across to Japan.

Herbert Spencer developed a philosophy that was very physicalist. In his discussion of human society he used physicalist concepts – terms such as 'conservation of force', and the 'evolution' and 'dissolution' of systems. For example, he wrote:

"Evolution under its simplest and most general aspect is the integration of matter and concomitant dissipation of motion; while Dissolution is the absorption of motion and concomitant disintegration of matter." (5)

Spencer also allowed for a god – he talked of the 'unknowable'. But mainly he was talking about the world one could find out about – and in very physical terms. An important thing to realise is that Spencer had a very strong influence. During the 1850s and 1860s, when such philosophy was taken very seriously, many people of influence, across the world, listened to Herbert Spencer. At the same time utilitarianism was becoming an influential moral philosophy.

In that context various people studying economics began to use physicalist ideas, as well as the concept of utility, to try to understand economics. They were people such as Stanley Jevons, Leon Walras, and Alfred Marshall. They began to think very seriously, in looking at how a market economy functions, in terms of the concept of utility and also in terms of using mathematics to understand what is going on, mathematics that was being used to analyse physical systems. In doing so they were trying to be what they thought was scientific. Moreover there was a theory of physics, concerning energy, proposed by Helmholtz which became very influential in their thinking (6).

What Jevons did, and what Walras did independently, was take the concept of utility and apply it very strictly to the market, or so they thought. They considered utility to be something that exists, and also that one can consider it to be a 'quantity' – that one can have more or less of it. Then they argued that that means one can use the mathematical calculus on it. So that is what they did. I will quote Jevons:

"It is clear that Economics, if it is to be a science at all, must be a mathematical science. There exists much prejudice against attempts to introduce the methods and language of mathematics into any branch of the moral sciences. Many persons seem to think that the physical sciences form the proper sphere of mathematical method, and that the moral sciences demand some other method, - I know not what. My theory of Economics, however, is purely mathematical in character. Nay, believing that the quantities with which we deal must be subject to continuous variation, I do not hesitate to use the appropriate branch of mathematical science, involving though it does the fearless consideration of infinitely small quantities. The theory consists in applying the differential calculus to the familiar notions of wealth, utility, value, demand, supply, capital, interest, labour, and all the other quantitative notions belonging to the daily operations of industry. As the complete theory of almost every other science involves the use of that calculus, so we cannot have a true theory of Economics without its aid." (7).

Then, believing that they could legitimately apply the calculus to the concept of utility, independently at around the same time, Jevons and Walras came to the same conclusion – each believed that they had proved that the 'free market', with no interference from outside, maximises the utility of the whole community of buyers and sellers involved. Their mathematics, their use of calculus, showed this, or so they thought.

This belief became very influential. It seemed to show that the free market, left to its own devices, reaches an equilibrium position where the utility of the community as a whole is maximised. Thus the neoclassical economists thought they had shown, from their mathematics, on a scientific basis, that the free market works best and should not be interfered with. That was their belief. It is a very erroneous one.

There is a great deal wrong with their argument about markets maximising utility. Utility is a badly defined concept, supposed to be the property of an object, but having psychological properties and referring to various different things. Also, although one could talk (perhaps) in terms of greater or lesser utility, it is a mathematical fallacy to believe that therefore one can use the calculus. The mathematical study of 'abstract algebra' shows that specific belief to be completely invalid (8).

However, Walras and Jevons did not realise that their application of calculus, to 'utility', was invalid. They thought they were being scientific. Furthermore their thinking is also based upon the belief that the 'free market' behaves very much like a physical system. They even compared it to physical systems in which energy is maximised.

The point is that to think one can apply calculus to the concept of utility is to be seriously wrong in so many ways – scientifically, mathematically, and psychologically. It cannot be done. However neoclassical economics has been the dominant economic theory for a hundred and fifty years. It did have a variant, Keynesian economics, that worked better for a while, but from the 1970s and 1980s Keynes' ideas were believed to be seriously flawed, and neoclassical economics returned. There had also been alternative economic views which were proposed and had influence in the 1890s, but whose influence waned (9).

If one comes back to 2009, and Paul Krugman's article, it is important to understand that modern economists are the direct descendents of Jevons and Walras. Thus in the later twentieth and early twenty-first centuries the financial markets were deregulated in the belief that the markets worked best when not regulated. This belief goes back to the 1860s and the arguments by Jevons and Walras about the supposed maximisation of utility.

So what has happened is that some thinking, that is based upon ideas of science that come from Newtonian physics, has been applied incorrectly to the human world. It is believed to be scientific. Even now there are people believing neoclassical economics to be scientific.

To me this is a very noteworthy demonstration of how ideas can be very powerful, and how ideas can take hold of people and affect how they think and behave. Of course, there can be other reasons why people adopt neoclassical economics and argue that the free market does not need to be regulated, because that allows them to do what they want within it. There can be all sorts of rationalisations involved. (The unregulated free market can also be believed to be the only alternative to Marxism or some other form of totalitarianism.)

However, at heart, neoclassical economics is based upon incorrect mathematics applied to utility. Furthermore utility is also a moral concept that, ironically, can rationalise immoral behaviour, especially craving. This is of note from a Buddhist point of view. Interestingly, if one investigates the behaviour of financiers and stock market traders it is very easy to come across highly addictive behaviour typifying intense craving, as the documentary film 'Inside Job' shows clearly.

So what happened was, and is, people applying physicalist ideas about science to the human world, to human behaviour. Those particular ideas about science, though very physicalist, also possessed some underlying theistic assumptions about providence, about God's natural laws being positive.

However, during the nineteenth century other ideas about science and about society were developing. In particular, there was what I have come to call 'social evolutionism', but which others have called 'social Darwinism' (10). Let us study another quotation. I wonder if you can guess which part of the political spectrum it is from, and when it was written:

"We know now that in natural selection at the stage of development where the existence of civilised mankind is at stake, the units selected from are not individuals, but societies... The French nation was beaten in the last war, not because the average German was an inch and a half taller than the average Frenchman, or because he had read five more books, but because the German social organism was, for the purposes of the time, superior in efficiency to the French. If we desire to hand on to the after world our direct influence, and not merely the memory of our excellence, we must take even more care to improve the social organism of which we form part, than to perfect our own individual developments. Or rather, the perfect and fitting development of each individual is not necessarily the utmost and highest cultivation of his own personality, but the filling, in the best possible way, of his humble function in the great social machine."

This quote is from 1889 and the author is Sidney Webb. It is from one of the 'Fabian Essays'. Sidney Webb was a founder member of the Fabian Society, which became part of the Labour Party in Britain. He is using terms like 'natural selection' and 'social organism' and he is referring to war. He is referring to one 'social organism' having been more efficient, better, than others.

This was a very common way of thinking in 1889. From the middle of the nineteenth century to the middle of the twentieth century, to think in terms of evolution, in terms of natural selection, and to think in terms of struggle, war and strife, was more or less standard. These ideas developed from earlier in the nineteenth century. At the beginning of that century Europe was being convulsed by a series of wars. There were the French revolutionary wars, which turned into the Napoleonic wars, when Napoleon came to power in France. There was also rapid industrialisation going on. There were major changes in society, and people were thinking in terms of 'struggle' and 'strife' because it was happening around them. They were beginning to think also that there was something positive, even moral, in struggle and strife, which somehow improved people and improved society. Some started to argue persuasively that war is a vital means to keep nations morally healthy. Thus the Prussian philosopher Hegel wrote: *"as the motion of the winds keeps the sea from stagnation, to which it would succumb by constant stillness, just as would nations by an enduring peace, let alone peace everlasting"*. Such ideas were associated with the belief that the individual *"achieves objectivity, truth, and morality, only so far as he is a member of the state"* (11).

Also, at the beginning of the nineteenth century, a Frenchman, Lamarck, came up with the idea of the evolution of species. He said that species had evolved, and he had a theory about how that happened. He hypothesised that there are two forces responsible, a 'complexifying force' and an 'adaptive force'. Moreover he thought that a crucial aspect of the latter was that individual members of a species, through practice, developed a skill, or developed themselves physically, in some way, and that they passed that improved skill, or improved physical aspect, on to their descendants. This is sometimes referred to as the theory of 'evolution through acquired characteristics' (12). It is interesting, as well, to note Lamarck's physicalist terminology.

It was Lamarck who came up with the idea of evolution. But it was 'in the air' already, as people were thinking in terms of progress, with respect to society. Other biologists had also come tantalisingly close to the idea of evolution of species. Then through the nineteenth century the idea of evolution took an increasing hold over people's thinking. I have already mentioned that Herbert Spencer talked in terms of evolution as applied to various aspects of existence. This included the realm of physics, the world of biological nature, and the human world. Importantly, the idea of evolution grew increasingly influential in consideration about the development or progress of human societies.

Nevertheless there had been someone who had argued against evolution at the end of the eighteenth century, or rather had argued against the idea of progress, at least in human society. That man was Malthus. He came up with an argument that implied that there could be in some way no progress. Malthus argued that there is no point giving much help in welfare and aid to the poor. The reason he gave was that they would only have more children, the population would therefore expand, and one would get yet more people who were poor. So do not do it, for if one gave them food it would just lead to them reproducing more and one will be 'back to square one', but with a larger population of poor people (13).

Malthus' argument was very influential. It seemed so logical. One of its effects was later on, in the 1830s, when there was a change of the welfare system in Britain. The old Elizabethan poor laws were overturned and a new workhouse system put in place, which was a very authoritarian and demeaning system meant to discourage people from seeking welfare benefits.

Malthus' ideas had major influence in other ways. There were a couple of people considering the evolution of species who thought about Malthus and this 'struggle for survival' amongst the poor, and about struggle for survival generally. Those two people were Charles Darwin and Alfred Wallace, who independently came up with a new theory of the evolution of species. By the mid-nineteenth century each had worked out the theory that there is an evolution of species through 'natural selection'. This theory assumes, that because of the 'struggle for survival' amongst individuals in a species (with there always being a struggle for survival in some way), and because there are naturally occurring variations within a species, that just as breeders can select variants of animals or plants and thereby change the nature and variety of a species, nature can do the same, i.e. can make selections through this process of struggle.

In other words, those individuals in a species that possess a variation in some way that allows them to survive longer, and have more offspring that survive, are the ones being in effect 'selected'.

Before that theory was proposed the evolution of species had been an idea that was growing in influence. But from the time when Darwin and Wallace jointly proposed their theory, evolution was taken very seriously indeed, especially with Darwin's presentation of evidence for evolution. This included the realisation that species evolution actually happened. Very importantly it was realised that human beings were the descendants of animals.

Of course, the evolution of species is a fact. But the interesting thing about the ideas that were proposed about evolution was that certain of those ideas came from the general political and philosophical thinking of the time. Moreover, Darwin did not come up with the idea of evolution, or the idea of struggle, at all. What he (and Wallace) had added was the idea that variations occurred naturally, and that natural circumstances could implicitly favour some variations rather than others, just as breeders explicitly made selections of the variations they particularly wanted.

A particular term that became attached to the theory of evolution by natural selection, was this one – 'survival of the fittest'. This phrase was coined by Herbert Spencer, after he had encountered Darwin's writings. Darwin incorporated the term into later editions of his book 'The Origin of Species'. When he used the phrase, 'Survival of the fittest', he only meant that the 'fittest' were just those that happen to have a variation that allowed them to propagate more successfully. But Spencer did not mean that, and other people came to see it in the way that Spencer saw it. The 'fittest' came to mean those who are superior, who are best – morally best, intellectually best, culturally best. People came to see evolution as being about survival of the fittest in this sense.

Importantly, this concept was taking hold of people when there was continuing strife between the nations of Europe, and when there were developing nation states with increasingly sophisticated weapons. So people came to think in terms of evolution as a struggle between variations, or types, of the same species, and they came to see human interactions, particularly between different human groups, as typifying the 'survival of the fittest'. People also became quite frightened by these ideas which influenced them in various ways.

Let us consider Germany for example. Actually Germany did not exist at the beginning of the nineteenth century, although there was the idea of the 'volk', meaning a distinct German people, that had been begun by Herder. Politically there was Prussia and various small German states. There was no overall German state. Furthermore, Prussia had been attacked by Napoleon. As the century progressed German speakers became concerned to develop a German nation that could survive and propagate itself. Such thinking continued after Germany was founded as a nation state. With hindsight one can understand where such thinking was leading.

Herbert Spencer had also used the term 'social organism'. People came to see nations as social organisms for which natural selection applied. This type of thinking was very influential. However, the ideas of struggle for survival, and natural selection, were also brought into free market economics – with enthusiasts stating it was the free market which was the way in which selection happened. This became another way of rationalising the idea that there should not be much of a welfare system, as this would only encourage the propagation of the least fit.

So what developed were some very powerful ideas about how evolution was happening in human society. Different people had different ideas about what the details of natural selection were, and whether it was individuals or the 'social organism' it worked upon, but they all had the idea that natural selection brought about the best result, and that evolution was a matter of progress to that best result. Herbert Spencer himself believed that there would be an evolution of society until it reached an 'equilibrium' point of the greatest happiness, and that that would come especially through a process of free trade. He also believed that in this process warfare would die away.

In contrast, other people believed that there had to be a struggle between different social organisms in order for somebody to come out on top - or, if they did not engage, they would be wiped out. There is a sad irony here, for the situation in nineteenth century Europe seems to resemble very much the situation of our hunter gatherer ancestors, but given extra impetus by ideas about evolution. The discovery of, and theorising about, evolution led to increased inter-group insecurity.

There was much fear in Germany, for example, that if they did not found colonies then they would disappear from the world stage. In Germany too, and in many other countries, people were becoming increasingly concerned about matters of ethnicity and race. Whilst considering one's own ethnic group superior, and others inferior, is a widespread human trait with a long history, the ideas about evolutionary struggle appear to have intensified it. Ethnic nationalism became a very strong current in people's thinking.

Thus there developed powerful ideas about the natural selection of the 'social organism' that constituted a nation state, and that it is very important for the nation state to show who is fittest by engaging in struggle with the others, in one way or another.

Furthermore, people had other ideas about what should be done about the supposed threats from the evolutionary struggle. Towards the end of the nineteenth century the idea of 'eugenics' developed. Eugenics is the belief that you should take action so that the 'most fit' members of society are those who propagate their offspring, and also discourage or ban other people, who are supposedly the 'least fit', from reproducing. Eugenics societies sprang up to promote such policies (14).

In general such ideas spread throughout the political spectrum. People very firmly held to these ideas about human evolution, with very strong emotions and fears attached to them. The outbreak of World War One happened in this context. It was not just that human beings were doing what they had always done, wage war with each other; it was not just that the technology of warfare had increased, and become much more sophisticated; but also, that at that time, in the

Western world and across to Japan, there were very influential and widely believed ideas about natural selection and its application to the human world.

So what was happening at the end of the nineteenth century and beginning of the twentieth, was that as well as physicalist ideas being applied to the world, there were also powerfully influential ideas derived from, or related to, biology being applied to the human world, in very harmful ways. It must be noted, however, that those ideas that came from biology themselves originated in part from the general political and philosophical thinking of the early nineteenth century. Then, as the twentieth century progressed, up to and beyond the outbreak of the First World War, these ideas became increasingly strong in their effects.

After the First World War there were some very disgruntled nations, Germany, Japan, and Italy in particular. Germany was the loser, and was penalised severely. The other two were technically on the 'winning side' in that war, but their requests were turned down at the post-war Versailles Conference. All three had been late entrants into the international world of nation states and colonialism. All three came away from that conference feeling humiliated and resentful. In that atmosphere, with continued fear, the ideas of natural selection and struggle took hold even more strongly. People in these three countries felt very threatened, both by the dominant Western powers, and also by the rise of communism. Consequently there was the rise of fascism in Italy, of Nazism in Germany, and of a fascist state in Japan (15).

There were also other factors contributing to the rise of fascism, such as the widespread belief that the two major forms of politics – liberal capitalism and communism, had failed. Fascism was seen as a 'third way' which allowed individual people to express themselves fully by participating in a nation state that took on an almost religious significance. It also emphasised the non-rational aspects of the human mind, and was critical of the materialism and supposed rationalism of the other two political perspectives.

Nazism, if one looks at it, is very much about the supposed superiority of one particular social organism, one particular ethnic group, the Germans. But that idea, central to Nazism, was not invented by the Nazis and nor was it unique to them. It had a long history. The rise of such political philosophy led directly to the Second World War. There is a desperate irony and sadness to the two world wars. They were replays of that old hunter-gatherer dilemma – what does one do about the threat, explicit or implicit, from other groups – reinforced by beliefs about evolution and 'survival of the fittest'.

After World War Two it is noteworthy that people in the Western world seem to have reacted strongly against thinking about social evolution, strife, and related ideas. One of those ideas, social evolutionism, involves what is now called 'racism', the belief that there are superior races and inferior races. Indeed, the concept of 'racism' can be understood as stemming from the reaction against social evolutionist views. In general, after World War Two, in the history of the last sixty years, those ideas have been discredited – although they may be resurfacing.

So, to summarise, there was a second aspect of nineteenth century scientism which took hold of the political world – the idea of evolution – along with the other idea that the laws of physics can be translated into the human world. It is important to recognise that these ideas came to be embedded in political beliefs across the political spectrum.

Herbert Spencer himself believed that society would evolve to a best possible point of 'equilibrium'. He thought this would happen through free trade. Others thought it would happen through warfare, with the superior race proving its superiority and establishing a thousand year Reich, or whatever. In general people believed there was a natural end result to the progress or evolution of society and culture; they believed it would happen more or less automatically. In other words they believed, in one way or another, that there was a determinate progression or evolution to the human world. Such a belief goes back at least to Augustine, although it was given extra impetus by the discovery of species evolution.

That type of belief, that there is some determinate process through which society evolves, perhaps through struggle, was also central to the thinking of Karl Marx. The Communist Manifesto, written by Marx and Engels, is from 1848, a time when ideas about evolution were common, especially ideas that society could progress in particular ways to a particular end point.

Marxism can be seen as being very fully part of this world of ideas. Marxism is sometimes called 'historical materialism'. The underlying implication is that physical or material factors are those which are most important in human history, in the human world. Marx himself had become an atheist. He did his PhD on ancient Greek atomic theory. He came to the conclusion that physical or material factors were most important in their effects on the human world, on human behaviour and belief. This was not just an atheist and materialist philosophy, but there was a further meaning to the term 'materialism'. Marx, in using this term, was referring to the 'means of production', the technology and manufacturing by which material goods are made and processed. In a way, one could put it that Marx's view of the dependence of human social and cultural behaviour on such 'material factors' paralleled the belief that the human mind was dependent upon, or identical to, the activity of the brain.

Marx came to believe that material factors were the most influential things underlying human society, and also that naturally there was a process of progress or evolution of society to a particular point. That progress came through struggle. For Marxism the struggle was between 'classes', the proletariat and the bourgeoisie. The positive end result, for Marx, was that society would evolve to a particular point where the bourgeoisie would be pushed aside, through armed struggle, and the proletariat would then become dominant, and somehow government, and everything that was negative, would wither away. So he believed that human beings could get to this utopia through the process of struggle between different groups, although not ethnic groups but social classes. In the Communist Manifesto Marx and Engels wrote: "*The proletariat of each country must, of course, first of all settle matters with its own bourgeoisie.*" They also wrote that the "*more or less veiled civil war*" between proletariat and bourgeoisie develops into "*the violent overthrow of the bourgeoisie*". They proposed that this violent process would bring about a utopia in which "*we shall have an association, in which the free development of each is the condition for the free development of all*". *(16)*

It is evident that Marxism is very much part of the nineteenth century way of thinking about human society in physicalist terms, as well as in terms of a set progression, with struggle and strife seen as part of that process of progression or evolution. Ironically too, Marx developed his theories influenced by Malthus' argument about the poor. This came about through Marx following the economist Ricardo's 'labour theory of value', with Ricardo's theory being based upon acceptance of Malthus' argument (17).

Looking at the nineteenth century in this way I found it extraordinary how strongly physicalist and 'social evolutionist' ideas were held, and how influential they were. It is very sobering to consider this, particularly given the history of the twentieth century. As well as the two world wars, the second of which included the Holocaust and some very nasty colonialism such as that in the Congo, there was also the rise of communism, based upon Marxist beliefs dating back to the mid-nineteenth century. It also became very apparent that communist revolutions did not lead at all to the withering away of political power, and to the free association of all, but to their complete opposites, despotic governments enslaving, starving, torturing and murdering their own citizens.

In Buddhist terms, looking at Marxism, there is a very important aspect of it, which is that Marx argued that things like culture and morality were just manifestations of the supposed 'material factors' and did not have any inherent validity. Ideas such as 'rights' and 'liberty' could simply be dismissed as just the rationalisations of the bourgeoisie. Associated with this dismissal, typically Marxists have also dismissed any systems of ideas except their own as being 'ideologies', whilst believing that Marxism, in contrast, is 'scientific'. In the Communist Manifesto Marx and Engels wrote, referring to the 'proletarian': "*Law, morality, religion, are to him so many bourgeois prejudices, behind which lurk in ambush just as many bourgeois interests.*" Thus Marxists, and communists in particular, did not have to take into consideration those ideas – in particular ideas about morality. As for the individual, the Communist Manifesto equates this idea with the "*middle class owner of property*" and goes on: *"This person must, indeed, be swept out of the way, and made impossible." (18)*

I emphasise that this is something which it is very important to consider in Marxism. Under Marxist governments there were around one hundred million people who died, that is, people killed by the actions of their own governments, which were Marxist regimes. I strongly suspect that that is because Marxism dismisses morality as just a rationalisation, and that actually what is implicitly good is what gets you to the supposed Marxist utopia. I will quote a Marxist:

"Hatred as the central element of our struggle! Hatred that is intransigent...hatred so violent that it propels a human being beyond his natural limitations, making him a violent and cold-blooded killing machine... We reject any peaceful approach. Violence is inevitable. To establish Socialism rivers of blood must flow! The imperialist enemy must feel like a hunted animal wherever he moves. Thus we'll destroy him! These hyenas are fit only for extermination. We must keep our hatred alive and fan it to paroxysm! The victory of Socialism is well worth millions of atomic victims!

To send men to the firing squad, judicial proof is unnecessary...These procedures are an archaic bourgeois detail. This is a revolution! And a revolutionary must become a cold killing machine motivated by pure hate."

That was written by the Cuban communist revolutionary, Che Guevara (19). So as a Buddhist I consider that it is very important that, if we are thinking about ideas and how influential they can be, then we recognise that they can be expressions of, and also encourage, very strong immorality. In particular Marxism is the embodiment of hatred, although it shares that distinction with ethnic nationalism, Nazism and fascism (as well as much tribal religion).

If we turn from Marxism to social evolutionism, we can see immorality coming from the idea of 'survival of the fittest', and that one ethnic group has got to fight, to prove that they are the fittest and that others are inferior. In Marxism, there is a similar logic. Both encourage and express hatred and the violence that stems from it. It is also of note that psychopaths became the leading figures in both political movements.

Meanwhile, in beliefs about the 'free market', competition in the free market is considered acceptable, and one can do what one likes, as the community's utility is supposedly maximised. In effect, it is believed that just by engaging in the 'market' everything will come out right. Of course it does not. Such beliefs encourage and express craving, indifference and exploitation. The appending of a variety of social evolutionist ideas onto free market beliefs also strengthened these beliefs.

In general, these ideas have been very powerful, and very damaging in their effects, because of their implicit or explicit encouragement of immorality. The belief that they are based upon science has contributed to the strength with which they were held. People with these ideas have looked to science, or what they understood science to be, and applied it to the human world. This has given a justification, or rationalisation, for behaving as they have.

This brings me to a question – as we are in the twenty-first century, in general what is the state of thinking *now* in the political and economic world? Is the state of our thinking still effectively back in the nineteenth century?

In answer to that question I would say, emphatically, that we are still thinking in nineteenth century terms. In general there seems to be a rigidity which has developed in modern Western political and economic thought, which is still dominated by old, extremely limited and very harmful ideas that developed in the nineteenth century. It is time to move on, for example using some twenty-first century science such as complexity theory, as well as applying Buddhist ideas and understanding.

5

The Restricted Choice

In this chapter I will look at how there has developed in Western thought what I have come to call 'the restricted choice'. This is the restricted choice of 'god or nothing', or of 'god or nothing but physical matter'. With regard to religion, this manifests in the common assumption that religion must either involve belief in some creator god ruling the universe, or else the only real alternative is to be an 'atheist' in the sense that that term has come to be used, meaning someone who believes in no religion, and that there is no spiritual dimension to the universe, and who usually also believes that the universe is made up of just physical matter.

As a Buddhist I am neither a theist, since I do not believe in a creator god who rules the universe, and nor am I an 'atheist' in the way that term is usually applied. I believe very strongly that there is what one could term a spiritual dimension to the universe, and that the universe is not reducible to physical matter. Even if I were not a Buddhist I would be neither a theist nor an atheist with the usual meaning of that term.

In my previous chapters I have discussed how science developed in the west in a theistic, Christian, context. Also, what developed were the *physical* sciences, in particular physics itself, with Newton's laws of motion, and, later on, biology. As I have discussed, this history of the rise of physical science within a theistic background was associated with the belief that there are natural laws underlying the world, and that those laws are god's laws. So Isaac Newton's laws of motion were seen as god's natural laws.

By the later nineteenth century one could say that western thought was dominated by two factors. There was still theism, although it had undergone changes in ideas and practices, and there was physical science. When people considered other aspects of the world, for example the human world, including areas such as economics and psychology, their thinking was dominated by those two factors – physical science and theism. Importantly, as I have discussed, physicalism developed, that is the belief that the human world has underlying laws similar to those of physics.

By the mid-nineteenth century many people held a view of the universe that one could characterise as 'god and physical matter'. People believed in god, but their thinking was very influenced by physicalism. There were influential philosophies promoted at that time, one of which I have mentioned before, the philosophy of Herbert Spencer. His philosophy combined two factors – in the main very physicalist ideas, but there was also a theistic strand which he called 'the unknowable'. His physicalism was linked to this. Thus he wrote that: *"In other words, asserting the persistence of Force, is but another mode of asserting an Unconditioned Reality, without beginning or end."* (1).

Another person who used such a combination of ideas, that is 'god and physical matter', was Francis Edgeworth. He wrote a book called 'Mathematical Psychics'. This was not about the application of algebra to séances but about applying mathematics to human psychology and human behaviour. It is instructive to consider two quotes from this book:

"The application of mathematics to the world of the soul is countenanced by the hypothesis (agreeable to the general hypothesis that every psychical phenomenon is the concomitant, and in some sense the other side of a physical phenomenon), the particular hypothesis adopted in these pages, that Pleasure is the concomitant of Energy. Energy may be regarded as the central idea of Mathematical Physics: maximum energy the object of the principle investigations in that science."

'Mechanique Sociale' may one day take her place along with 'Mechanique Celeste,' throned each upon the double-sided height of one maximum principle, the supreme principle of moral as of physical

science. As the movements of each particle, constrained or loose, in a material cosmos are continually subordinated to one maximum sum-total of accumulated energy, so the movements of each soul, whether selfishly isolated or linked sympathetically, may continually be realising the maximum energy of pleasure, the Divine love of the universe."

So Edgeworth was a theist who also thought in very physicalist terms. He believed that there were natural laws underlying the human world, which he referred to as 'mechanique sociale', social mechanics, which are like those applying in the physical world, 'mechanique celeste' or celestial mechanics. Furthermore he related a specific theory about maximising physical energy to what he considers to be a closely related phenomenon which he believes to happen in the world of 'souls', the supposed maximisation of the 'energy of pleasure, the Divine love of the universe'.

Very clearly, this quote contains theistic ideas which are closely bound up with ideas derived from nineteenth century physics. There is also implicit reference to the study of thermodynamics, which was a prominent aspect of the physics of the time, as well as to an influential theory by Helmholtz about the energy of physical systems.

Moreover in this quote Edgeworth is actually referring implicitly to a particular academic discipline, which was his own. He was for nearly thirty years a professor of economics at Oxford University. The quote is referring to something I discussed in the previous chapter, the fallacious mathematical 'proof' that the 'free market' maximizes utility. So Edgeworth himself believed that the mathematics used had proven that the 'free market' worked in very much the way that physical systems worked, supposedly maximizing something (be it energy or utility, or pleasure), and thereby worked very much in everybody's best interest.

Now I have mentioned two people who combined physicalism and theism. Both were theists to some extent or other. However that physicalist way of thinking also gradually became divorced from theism. Beginning in the eighteenth century people started to become agnostic or atheist. This became increasingly common in the nineteenth century, especially when scientific discoveries such as the evolution of species contradicted the Bible, which undermined many people's faith in the Bible, and their belief in a god.

Many people did not know quite where they were with regard to religion. They became agnostic. But others quite consciously dropped theism and often reacted strongly against it – these were the atheists.

There is something that is of particular note in the development of atheist thought – which is that from early on the atheists adopted a materialist view of the universe. In other words they believed that everything was made up of physical matter, and that if one understood physical matter one could understand everything. Thus atheists were like theists who were physicalist, but they went further, and in relinquishing belief in a god they adopted a very strict materialist belief system.

At first there were very few atheists – in the eighteenth century a few people here and there. One was Baron D'Holbach, one of the encyclopaedists. He was an atheist when it was still quite a difficult thing to be, but at least one did not get killed for it. D'Holbach wrote this:

"*The universe, that vast assemblage of every thing that exists, presents only matter and motion: the whole offers to our contemplation nothing but an immense, an uninterrupted succession of causes and effects.*" (3)

He was stating what is actually a belief, that everything that exists is made up of physical matter and its motion. It was an important part of his atheism. He was not just denying that there is a god. He was also stating that everything that exists is only made up of physical matter. There is no basis whatsoever for him to say that, but he was stating it nevertheless.

It is important to realise, that the belief that the universe is just made up of physical matter is just that, a belief. It grew up as an aspect of the rejection of theism.

By the nineteenth century such thinking was common. For example, in the earlier nineteenth century there was another Frenchman, Auguste Comte. He developed a system of thought called 'positivism'. Comte's positivism was based upon the physical sciences and, again, the belief that one could discover laws in the human world that were similar to laws in the physical world.

Comte believed that there are three stages to the development of human society, or at least to the development of thinking about the world. Earliest was what he termed the 'theological' stage where people believed that things existed, were created, or changed, because there are supernatural entities, such as 'spirits' or 'gods' of some sort or other. Comte said that theological thinking gradually developed into the idea of there being just one god. He believed that this stage developed into a 'metaphysical' stage, where, instead of talking in terms of gods or spirits, people started to understand phenomena as being due to abstract causes - thus a tree grew, not because of a god or tree spirit, but due to having a 'vegetative soul'. Comte's third and last stage of development was what he termed the 'positive' stage, where human beings understand the laws of cause and effect that control the world (4).

Comte also believed that these laws of cause and effect apply to the human mind. Like Baron D'Holbach he understood the human mind to be something that was either just a physical thing, somehow made up of physical matter and its motion, or somehow caused by it. Comte thought that the laws of the mind would be found through studying anatomy and physiology.

So, again, there is the idea that one can understand the human world, in fact human beings themselves, and the human mind, through studying the physical world. By the mid-nineteenth century and through the latter half of the nineteenth century these atheist, materialist ideas got stronger and stronger in influence. I quoted two theistic views of the time, but materialist atheist authors' books became best sellers in the latter half of the nineteenth century. For example, a German author, Karl Vogt, sold 100,000 copies of his books in various

European languages. He became known for statements like *'thoughts come out of the brain as gall from the liver, and urine from the kidneys'*. In other words, our thoughts are physical things just like gall and urine.

Another bestselling author was also a German, named Ludwig Buchner. He wrote a popular book, called 'Force and Matter', in which he said that the only forces in the world are associated with matter, so that there is no such thing as a spiritual force – everything is reducible in the end to physical matter and the physical forces that go with it (5).

So, by the latter half of the nineteenth century, thought in Europe was very much influenced by the physical sciences. This is unsurprising, as the physical sciences were discovering more and more, and the technology that came from these discoveries was transforming the world. It is very understandable that people were thinking in those terms. But the point that needs emphasis is that people made too much of those physical discoveries. In doing so they made two mistakes, one being the development of physicalist ideas, the other being the establishment of materialist philosophy.

It is understandable that people became impressed by the physical sciences, and also that this undermined their belief in the existence of a creator god. However, they went a step too far in believing that the increasing success of the physical sciences somehow proved that the universe is just made up of physical matter. This further, materialist, belief went with rejection of anything seen as 'superstition' (an attitude which is still typical of 'atheists' today). Ironically there seem to be implicit old Christian attitudes underlying such atheist belief – it certainly parallels a Christian rejection of 'paganism'. Moreover there is an emphasis on rational thought, within physicalism and materialism, which results in the downplay and denigration of myths and symbols. This is an interesting parallel with the extreme Protestant rejection of ritual.

Not only did physicalism become highly influential, but also materialism became an entrenched belief in much of the western world. As time went on what developed in western thought was a restricted range of ideas (though there are exceptions) with the dominant beliefs being on the one hand Christian or theistic thinking and on the other hand materialist philosophy. An important consequence of this is that in considering any particular area, any particular field of enquiry, people have come to think in these terms, either 'God or matter', or sometimes 'god and matter' – that is the apparent choice - for understanding anything.

People implicitly apply this restricted choice when they try to understand Buddhism. So if someone is trying to think about Buddhism it is typical for them to try to categorise it as belonging to one of those categories – either it is a religion like Christianity and so has got to be theist, or it must be a form of atheist materialism. How could it not be either of these? But Buddhism is very definitely neither.

I have come across quotes from Christian authors (from a hundred years ago) describing Buddhism as a form of nihilistic materialism, and I can remember discussing with acquaintances who learned I was a Buddhist and who said 'that's just like Christianity; you believe in things like god'. People cannot understand there being a possibility of there being anything different from those two views. This is very evident in mainstream debates touching on religious matters, or in which a religious viewpoint is sought. If one studies such debates, for example a debate in the newspapers or TV, what one typically finds is what I have come to call 'a bishop and a Dawkins' - on the one hand a bishop, and on the other, as a modern representative of atheists, usually Richard Dawkins. (I was amused, having just written this, to learn of a debate at the Cambridge University Student Union, with Richard Dawkins and Rowan Williams, the ex-Archbishop of Canterbury, as the main speakers, accompanied by some other humanists and theists).

If I listen to, or read, such debates I typically realise that I do not share any of the main assumptions of either side. I find myself thinking: 'What about us? And what about Buddhist ideas?' But the point is that the participants cannot really understand where Buddhism is coming from. Ironically both Dawkins and his theist opponents in debate share common assumptions.

So, in general there developed in western thought this restricted choice between god and nothing but matter. As I discussed before, the physicalism of the nineteenth century had various developments in the political world, and in economics. There are other developments from that time which I have not yet mentioned, which have also been very important.

For example, there were highly influential materialist and physicalist developments in the world of psychology and psychotherapy. In this regard I was trying to remember the basis of Freud's thinking, and then I recalled that I have an introduction to Freud and his thinking, written in the nineteen fifties. I therefore took it down from my bookshelves, dusted it off, and proceeded to look up in it what it called 'Freud's scientific legacy'. Within about ten seconds I came across this: *"There were other influences that affected Freud even more profoundly. These came from physics. In the middle of the century, the great German physicist, Hermann von Helmholtz, formulated the principle of the conservation of energy. This principle stated, in effect, that energy is a quantity just like mass is a quantity. It can be transformed but not destroyed...."* (6)

As the author of the book makes clear, that is one of the foundation ideas underlying Freudian theory and the therapy he developed, psychoanalysis. This is a physicalist idea, that energy is conserved, and that one cannot get rid of certain energies. If one studies Freudian thought it is clearly based upon such physicalism.

Consider another development. In western academic psychology there developed in the early twentieth century the approach called 'behaviourism'. This rested upon the assumption that it is not legitimate to talk about what is going on in the mind – that that is at best 'subjective', not 'objective', as one cannot see into someone's mind, if it exists at all. Behaviourists considered that mind most probably does not exist, but in any case it cannot be investigated 'objectively'. Furthermore they believed that all one can talk about and analyse is the behaviour that one can see and measure, and, although there might be physical things going on in the brain they cannot be seen either (at least in the early twentieth century), so psychology must consist of the study and measurement of behaviour.

It is sobering to realise what behaviourism developed into. The behaviourists thought that one could understand human psychology by putting rats into boxes and rewarding them with food for pressing levers, and they took that very seriously. My immediate reaction now to this belief is 'it's crazy – how can one possibly understand the complexities of human psychology by putting rats in boxes and giving them food if they press a lever?' But behaviourism, with its rats in boxes, was taken very seriously. And at heart behaviourism was based upon physicalist and materialist assumptions about what exists and how one should study it.

Another practice that developed, at more or less the same time that behaviourism developed, was in a different field, that of management. There grew up the practice of what became known as 'scientific management'. It started about a hundred years ago, and was associated with Harvard Business School and a man named Frederick Taylor.

There is a very disturbing book about management, called 'The Puritan Gift', which argues that 'scientific management' has led to a serious loss in the ability to manage, and that management ideas and practices throughout the twentieth century and into the twenty-first have become progressively subverted by ideas of management that are fundamentally unsound, which are argued to be developments from the work of Frederick Taylor (7). The book discusses management practice in America, and uses evidence for this from American businesses, but it also looks at other areas such as the armed forces, and health care. For example, in discussing the health service in America, it shows how this style of incompetent management had been very influential in healthcare. The authors wrote, contrasting the good hospital practice associated with Florence Nightingale with what replaced it:

"Nightingale's most famous dictum was that it is 'the very first requirement in a Hospital that it should do the sick no harm'. Thanks to the impact of the Cult of the (so-called) Expert, the typical American hospital fails that test. For the authors, the symbol of the new era has to be a half-eaten, dried out meal sitting for hours by a hospital bed occupied by a semi-conscious patient."

After I wrote the first draft of this essay I read about a report by an academic looking into social and nursing care in Britain, who was blaming management ideas and practices, from management courses, as being a major factor responsible for the serious lowering of care amongst nursing and social care staff. Since then the Francis Report has been published, which investigated the serious failings of a particular hospital, involving very many unnecessary deaths, and it is very evident reading it, that poor management is a serious issue not just in the hospital concerned, but also in the various organisations supposedly involved in regulating the quality of care at that hospital. Similar failings are evident elsewhere in the NHS. Actually in the Puritan Gift the authors mentioned that the 'typical British public-sector hospital' also fails the Nightingale test, and described the NHS as having abandoned the earlier Nightingale system due to the advice of a "neo-Taylorite 'scientific' manager…who went on to destroy the company which he chaired…" (8).

It is worrying that all too often modern management appears just not up to the job. Moreover, in particular areas, poor management kills. A vital question to ask is how much of current management practice is now affected by seriously flawed thinking stemming ultimately from 'scientific management'. Furthermore, how much have the understanding and skills of senior civil servants and politicians been adversely affected by imbibing poor management ideas and practices (as well as fundamentally flawed economic theories)?

To help one answer these questions it is worthwhile considering what 'The Puritan Gift' lists as crucial characteristics of the tradition of flawed management practice stemming ultimately from 'scientific management':- a preoccupation with measurement, including 'targets', rather than good qualitative knowledge; credence given to a manager's paper qualifications and certificates, rather than their level of 'domain knowledge' (i.e. real knowledge of the needs and practices of the specific business or organisation being managed); and 'top-down' control ignoring the expertise, knowledge and opinions of those lower down in the hierarchy (9). The use of 'outsourcing' and the establishment of an 'internal market' within a business or organisation, are also characteristics of this approach. Moreover, instead of there being a clear line of command, managers may have diffuse and unclear responsibilities, and 'experts', outside of any clear line of command, may be used to develop 'initiatives' to overcome problems. Personally I recognise several of these characteristics in how the National Health Service has been governed from above by politicians and Whitehall civil servants.

In general, what we can see in the twentieth and into the twenty-first centuries, in a variety of fields, is that physicalist, and at times materialist, ideas have had strong effects upon the human world. People have applied such ideas, often with disastrous effects.

Another area of importance, adversely affected by the restricted choice, is that of ethics or morality. Here the restricted choice has had its effects in a somewhat different way. Theistic ideas of morality are really that 'god makes laws' which people have to obey. For example, in the Bible are the 'Ten Commandments'. But if one stops believing in god, and one believes there is nothing but physical matter, what can then be the basis of one's moral philosophy? If morality is about 'laws', where does one find the laws? One is left with a serious problem.

In the last chapter I discussed utilitarianism, which was one attempt to develop a non-theistic moral philosophy. There also developed in the nineteenth century what has been called the 'agnostic morality', described thus: *"low key; not absolute; a conviction that we can be unselfish and that unselfish men are happy but that to be unselfish is difficult and can be fostered by family and by society, we must do the best we can by others so far as we may in these complicated circumstances"* (10). Agnostic morality is what one could describe as an offshoot of nineteenth century Christian morality but without any explicit reference to a god. Within it there can be the implicit sense that there is a moral dimension to behaviour, but there is no clear basis for understanding how this can be the case.

A very important development exhibiting the problem about non-theistic morality is what is called 'relativism', which I mentioned before. This is the idea that there is no objective morality in the world, with the corollary that any moral system is just a particular group's beliefs about what is right and wrong. Moreover, this is often taken further, with the added belief that there is not much to choose between different moral systems, as everybody's opinion is equally 'valid' – one just adopts the moral rules of one's group, and that is all they are, nothing objective. Relativism became very strong in the late twentieth century. It also has been accompanied by the further belief that one cannot criticise people from other cultures because one's criticism is just one's own cultural view; they have got their cultural view, and no one is better, as there is no objectively existing morality on which one can base ones criticism of anyone else's moral system.

This has led to very serious double standards, and to the de facto approval of highly immoral ideas and practices stemming from non-western cultures and religions. This can be accompanied by strong criticism of anything western.

Another way in the West that moral philosophy has developed is that it has more or less explicitly disappeared, but has re-appeared in disguise, as it were, in a different arena. It has become an implicit part of political thinking. So it can often be that people's ideas of what is right and wrong are very much bound up with their political views. In effect this is a form of relativism, for explicit moral philosophy has disappeared. Looked at another way it is accompanied by what one could call 'competing moral absolutisms', as members of each group strongly assert that they, and their group, are right. (Ironically the strong assertion of the rightness of one's political views can be accompanied by an explicit dismissal of there being an objectively existing morality. There is actually a link between moral absolutism, whether justified by reference to a supposed god or to one's political group, and relativism. One could even put it that they are two sides of the same coin.)

There is another way to consider moral philosophy, which goes back to the natural law tradition. Thus one could investigate the human world, especially human behaviour, and try to find out what natural moral laws there are. This is a very important tradition. As I discussed in my third chapter, human rights developed out of the idea that god created human beings and the human world, and had given people 'inalienable rights' and created them 'equal'. By the twentieth century, and the UN Declaration of Human Rights, god was explicitly dropped from that, and we just get the idea that there are human rights. As I have already mentioned, there is a very interesting irony that as relativism has grown, with people believing that there is no objectively existing morality, people have also taken the idea of human rights more and more seriously, and actually brought them into effect more. Perhaps one could call the doctrine of human rights an island of moral philosophy in a sea of relativism.

The crucial issue with the idea of natural laws is that if one drops the idea of god, one is left with a problem – if one is not a Buddhist. One could study people, and find out how people behave. One could discover, for example, how people make moral decisions. One could study that as thinkers in the eighteenth century did, such as David Hume or Adam Smith. Or one could study it as psychologists currently do. But studying what people do does not help decide what people should or should not do, how one should or should not act. It just describes what people do.

One could also put that study in the context of human evolution, and say that people have evolved having particular qualities and attributes, that they are in part selfish but also have altruistic attributes – evolution gives us both. From that one could say it is sensible for us all to act in an altruistic way because we would all be better off if we did so – and that argument has quite a lot going for it. But, for example, how does one answer the psychopath who says 'I'm not going to play like that. I enjoy hurting people. Why shouldn't I?' Stating that everyone is better off if all are altruistic is not enough to answer the psychopath's challenge of why they should not harm people. They can simply answer that they enjoy harming people, and 'so what?' if people get hurt. One is left with the major problem that the psychopath's question remains unanswered.

In general, western non-theist moral philosophy has been left with that major problem – if one does not believe in a god, how can there be a natural morality, or natural moral laws? This problem is exemplified by moral relativism, although such relativism is often accompanied by an implicit absolutism, especially concerning a person's own political views.

There is a further problem with trying to establish morality from the background of the restricted choice. If one ditches god, as it were, and one has only got physical matter, then if one looks at morality and realises that morality is intimately concerned with pleasure and pain, precisely how is the existence of pleasure and pain understood in that materialist view of the world?

If one goes back to those nineteenth century authors I mentioned, and the idea that thoughts are just manifestations of the physical nervous system, a bit like urine coming out of the kidneys, presumably they meant their arguments to apply to pleasure and pain as well. So are pleasure and pain just different modes of activity of the nervous system? *How* do they exist? Also, if one thinks about the mind in general, is it true that it is reducible to physical matter? So, if one is in pain, precisely how does that pain exist? Is the pain made up of atoms? Physical forces? Or what?

Or if one is smelling the smell of a rose, is that smell made up of atoms, or what? If one hears a sound, or sees a reddish colour chair, for example, what are those experiences made of? Does it make sense to say they are made up of atoms, or not?

What we are getting into is the crucial issue when Baron D'Holbach asserted that everything consists of physical matter, and people in the nineteenth century asserted the same belief. Is it *really* the case, that when we are talking about the mind, that the mind can be reduced to physical matter, to the activity of the brain?

Does it even make sense to say that things like one's experience of the smell of a rose, one's experience of pain, actually exist? That might seem like a foolish question, but I mentioned behaviourism which ruled such things out of court. In fact in the twentieth century many people in psychology and philosophy believed it was invalid to talk about people's internal conscious experience. I will quote from a philosopher, writing in the 1990s. The philosopher is John Searle, and the quote is from his book 'The Rediscovery of the Mind' (11). He is describing being a philosopher discussing the philosophy of consciousness with his students:

"When I read the standard authors and tried to explain their views to my students, I was appalled to discover that with few exceptions these authors routinely denied what I thought were simple and obvious truths about the mind. It was then, and still is common to deny, implicitly or explicitly, such claims as the following: We all have inner subjective qualitative states of consciousness…"

"Mainstream orthodoxy consists of various versions of 'materialism'…. What I argued for then and repeat here is that one can accept the obvious facts of physics – that the world consists entirely of physical particles in fields of force – without denying that among the physical features of the world are biological phenomena such as inner qualitative states of consciousness…"

"Mental phenomena are caused by neurophysiological processes in the brain, and are themselves features of the brain." (Chapter 1)

Let us unpack that. This is a contemporary philosopher. He is criticising materialists who believe that there are no internal states of consciousness, no inner experience at all. He is calling them materialists and implying that such a belief is nonsense, and that of course we all have internal states. But then he goes on to say that mental states, consciousness, are actually aspects of the nervous system, processes within brains, and that everything consists of physical particles and fields of force.

So Searle is a contemporary philosopher echoing what D'Holbach said in the eighteenth century, and what people like Comte and Vogt said in the nineteenth. He is echoing the belief that everything that exists is made up of physical atoms and fields of force. Nevertheless, he criticises the extreme materialist view that the internal conscious states do not exist at all.

The question to consider is whether the belief that mental states are just brain processes is actually true.

One can read materialist authors. They typically make the claim that this belief has been proven to be true. (A contemporary example is Daniel Dennett (12).) But it actually has never been proved, certainly not by Baron D'Holbach, nor in the nineteenth century, and it has not happened since. Yet materialists have believed it to be true. It is an irony that people who typically consider themselves to be rationalists, and who claim to base their thinking upon evidence, are actually asserting what is just a belief.

The crucial issue is whether the mind, consciousness, is reducible to physical matter, in particular the physical processes of the nervous system and brain. Is that the case? Now this is where thinking gets difficult. It is a very complicated topic to consider. But let us consider the issues a little.

Obviously we each have a physical nervous system and brain, within a physical body. But is that all?

Let us consider our visual experience. We have visual images of the world around us. A first, apparently foolish, question: is the visual image you have, of the world around you at this moment - is it an *image* of the world, or the world itself?

Of course, it is an image of the world. We know that in the physical world light comes from the objects around one, hits the retina of each eye, gets converted into electrical brain impulses which then give rise to a whole visual image of the world around one. So the physical world is, as it were, out there, leading to a series of processes, in one's physical body, to one's experience of the world around one.

If that is the case then the image of the world, at the end of the process, cannot be the same as the world itself, at the beginning of the process. The two are different. This seems obvious, but usually, as we go about the world, we take our image of the world to be the actual world itself. We do not go around thinking, for example, 'this is my visual image of my hand'. Instead, implicitly and automatically, we take the image to be the actual thing of which it is an image. Very importantly, we have to be clear about this distinction, which we do not usually make. If we do not make this distinction then it is very easy to become utterly confused about what is meant by 'inner qualitative states of consciousness', to use Searle's phrase.

Moreover, one's visual image of the world is integrated with information from other senses, for example the tactile sense. Thus one's overall image of one's hand has both a visual and a tactile image integrated together. Interestingly, experiments can be conducted in which people can be made to have very weird experiences of themselves and the world. For example, one can make people feel that an artificial hand is their hand - they apparently have feeling in an artificial hand. Their brain is constructing a combined visual and tactile image which is incorrect. One can also get people to wear a visual mask with a screen inside it, so that they do not see what is in front of them but what the screen shows them. The screen then shows what is being filmed from a camera behind them. So the visual image they experience comes from the viewpoint of the camera behind them. This gives them a sense of being out of their bodies. Their tactile sense of being where they are, and their visual sense, have become disconnected, and their brain has been tricked into constructing a virtual image of the world which is incorrect (13).

The point is that our sense experience, our sense consciousness, consists, at least in part, of a virtual world, one which also contains a multi-sensory image of oneself. We usually implicitly take it as being the actual physical world, but it is a virtual world, a constructed image based upon the physical world around us. But then there is the crucial question – of what is that virtual world, that sense consciousness, made? Is it really made up of brain impulses, as Searle asserts? Is that virtual world itself within the physical world, in particular within the brain? Let us consider these questions carefully.

Searle claimed that 'mental phenomena are caused by neurophysiological processes in the brain, and are themselves features of the brain.' If that is literally the case then presumably one's experience must itself be made up of features of the brain, or neurological processes. Also, if they really are literally the same, if one could in some way get inside the brain of a conscious person one would find those actual mental phenomena. Otherwise Searle's statement is nonsensical. So, what are the answers to these questions?

Now, at this moment in time do you have any actual conscious experience of various chemicals going in and out of myriads of nerve calls? Can you discriminate, in your current experience, all those bits of brain chemicals? Or even any collection of them? Is that what your experience is made up of? Well, obviously not. Mine certainly is not.

Moreover if, for example, someone is smelling a rose, and one could open up their brain, would the smell of a rose drift out? Well, no. If they were listening to music through headphones, if one opened up their brain would the sounds of that music be heard? Again, no. Parts of the brain have not literally turned into a smell or a noise.

The conclusion is straightforward. Our sense consciousness and our physical brain are not the same. If they were literally the same - if mental phenomena 'are themselves features of the brain' - the answers to those questions would have to be 'yes'. However materialist philosophers tend to avoid this conclusion by also claiming that sense consciousness is 'caused by' or 'arises from' the physical processes in the brain. Searle's statement is an example of this. Such a twofold assertion confuses the issues, and takes the spotlight away from the erroneous assertion that the phenomena of sense consciousness 'are' brain processes.

Moreover, materialist arguments that brain processes 'cause' or 'give rise' to sense consciousness also contain serious confusion. Indeed, whilst physical processes in the brain can be said to 'give rise' to conscious experience, with one specific meaning to the phrase 'give rise', materialists have no way whatsoever to explain how that happens. What they typically do is present confused arguments about how sense consciousness arises, which apparently explain away its independent existence.

Searle actually used the phrase 'mental phenomena are caused by neurophysiological processes…" There is an ambiguity in both the phrase 'give rise to', and even more so in the term 'caused by'. The ambiguity is about whether or not the processes which 'give rise to' or 'cause' something else are completely responsible for the existence of that something else. Something can 'cause' or 'give rise to' something else' but not be completely responsible for its existence. Thus, if a radio is tuned into a particular radio station then what is broadcast from the radio station 'causes' or 'gives rise to' what sounds come out of the radio. However, what is broadcast is not completely responsible for those sounds – there has to be a functioning radio as well, whose existence is independent of the existence of the radio station. Likewise, activity in the brain may 'give rise to' or 'cause' the contents of consciousness, but it is not completely or solely responsible for the existence of consciousness. Our consciousness may be 'tuned in', as it were, to our brain, but that does not mean that consciousness is an aspect of the brain. However, this point is typically overlooked in materialist arguments, and 'gives rise to' and 'causes' are confused with 'is completely responsible for the existence of'. Of course, brain activity often 'gives rise' to the phenomena of conscious experience, but there has to be what one could call a non-physical 'stream of consciousness' or perhaps an 'aware space', in which the phenomena occur. However, materialists deny, as an article of belief, that there can be anything non-physical.

I mentioned that they also typically have no explanation for how brain processes give rise to conscious experience, but instead 'explain away' its independent existence. One typical way for them to explain it away is to simply assert 'our inner sense experience is a physical process', just as John Searle has asserted this. But such an assertion is simply untrue. Another typical argument was used in what was called 'identity theory', i.e. the theory that consciousness and brain activity are 'identical'. This argument used the analogy of lightning (14). The argument went as follows: just as a flash of lightning is but the movement of charged physical particles through the air, so our conscious experience is the movement of particles in the nervous system. The crucial issue to realise with such an argument is that it smuggles in an observer who is different from the particles. Thus lightning, to be perceived as lightning, is perceived by a person external to it. Applying the analogy strictly means that the particles in the nervous system are observed by something or someone external to them, i.e. a non-material mind, the very thing the theory is arguing against.

What I wish to emphasise here is that materialist philosophers can never explain consciousness. There is just an enormous gap in any explanation they could give, at the point where they argue that physical processes 'give rise to' or 'cause' the phenomena of consciousness. If one starts off with materialist assumptions one cannot get to the phenomena of sense consciousness, no matter how hard one may try.

People find it very difficult to come to that conclusion. This is because of their strongly held *belief* that everything in the universe is, and must be, made up of physical matter and its accompanying forces.

Yet one is always left with a gap that materialism cannot explain. Of course, currently, nobody can explain it. Of what is consciousness made up? We do not have the concepts with which to answer the question. But the fact that we do not possess such concepts, and currently have no idea, does not mean that consciousness does not exist as a phenomenon distinct from physical matter.

Now materialism in western thought developed as an aspect of atheism, and is bound up with the western escape from theistic authoritarianism. But materialism is a philosophical position that really does not make sense.

It is very interesting to contemplate where we currently are in science and thought, compared with people in the nineteenth century, and with where people were a thousand years ago. A thousand years ago western thought was more or less two things – Catholic Christian thought with a mixture of Aristotle. That broke down. By the nineteenth century there was still some theism, but with physicalism and materialism coming in, which have together been dominant for a hundred and fifty years or more.

What I am beginning to wonder is whether we are on the threshold of another change, where physicalism and materialism are recognised to be fundamentally lacking when we are theorising about the human world, as people begin to realise the inadequacy of materialist explanations of consciousness, and as modern science overturns old physicalist ideas. Maybe also, as Buddhism is spreading to the West, people will be able to start thinking in very, very different ways to what they have been doing. So perhaps we are actually on the threshold of a very different way of thinking about the world, as different from nineteenth century scientism and theism, as that was from the old Christianity and Aristotle. Maybe we are on the cusp of something altogether different.

6

Buddhism, Psychology and Psychotherapy

The disciplines of psychology and psychotherapy began in the late nineteenth century, and when one studies their development it clearly reflects the influence of physicalism. If one goes back to the beginnings of psychology as a discipline in its own right, one is going back to people who wanted to apply the scientific methods of the time to the study of human beings. They were strongly influenced by the ideas around at the time.

What happened first of all was the founding of some university departments of psychology, in the later nineteenth century. What the psychologists there did was try to measure aspects of human psychology. For example, in German universities there were some people who were very keen to measure the strength of physical stimuli – such as the intensity of a light - and how that correlated with what a person actually sees, how strong the visual image of that light actually appears. I am referring here to people such as Wilhelm Wundt and Gustav Fechner. (1) These early psychologists did large numbers of experiments trying to find out the relationships between the actual physical intensity of stimuli, such as light or sound, and how people experienced them. Their work overlapped with the study of physiology. (Wundt's major book was actually entitled 'Physiological Psychology'.) This, for them, was being scientific about psychology, and they were very serious about such issues.

Something somewhat different occurred in one of the first American psychology departments, at Cornell University. This was due to a man named Edward Titchener. He was an Englishman. He was influenced by the scientific method of the psychologists in Germany, particularly by Wundt, but was very concerned to classify, as accurately and objectively as possible, the contents of our conscious experience – the actual structure of that experience. His approach has had various names, 'structuralism' and 'introspectionism' being two (2).

He considered that one had to take a special training to investigate consciousness, to introspect, in order to talk objectively about its structure and contents. For example, one could not say 'in my consciousness there is an image of a table'. One had to break the image down into its constituent aspects, and avoid making inferences based upon one's knowledge about what the image portrayed. Titchener took this procedure very seriously, and considered that this is where the science of psychology has to start, by studying the contents and structure of conscious experience in this way.

However Titchener was also concerned to deny common sense notions about consciousness or mind, which he lampooned as amounting to belief in an "insubstantial manikin living inside the head". He defined his subject matter as "experience dependent upon an experiencing person" and believed that that experience is itself dependent upon the nervous system.

When I was reading up on Titchener and his followers, it led me to make a comparison. They used their introspective method to study the nature and contents of consciousness, but Buddhists do something similar. When we are meditating we are becoming aware of the contents of our consciousness, developing an understanding of them, as well as trying to change them. In making that comparison I realised that Titchener and his followers did not have meditation. Then it occurred to me that one could compare what they were doing with what the Buddha himself did.

What then did the Buddha, the historical Buddha, actually do, as far as we can tell from the old Buddhist texts? It is clear from those texts that the Buddha went out alone into the wild, and he meditated, completely on his own. In other words he lived in a very different environment to Titchener and his followers, who would be leading very normal, everyday lives immersed in the world, and immersed in an academic department. In effect the Buddha was living 'on retreat' away from the myriad influences of daily life which affect one's mental state. (The importance of this is something which many meditators, who have experienced the difference between being 'on retreat' and being immersed in ordinary daily life, come to recognise).

What would the Buddha have been experiencing? He would have been meditating, exploring and developing his meditation practice as he went along. This would have involved a continued exploration of the nature and contents of consciousness, and of the qualities and attributes of mental states. Also, the Buddha's meditation had an ethical dimension to it, and he would have been discovering the effects of different motivations upon his mental state and behaviour. In reading the Buddhist texts the impression I get is that the Buddha started to dwell increasingly consistently in more and more concentrated, and ethically positive, states of consciousness. For example, the Buddha is likely to have been dwelling, at least all the time he was not asleep, in 'access concentration', if not going into the more deeply concentrated states called 'dhyana'. Access concentration is when one can hold the focus of one's attention for any length of time on what one wants to focus, without being distracted away from it.

Now if the Buddha was constantly in access concentration then that is actually a very helpful state to be in for exploring the contents of consciousness. This is because, as one begins to dwell consistently in access concentration, then various positive qualities of mind develop and strengthen, like the ability to work with one's mind, to have one's mind do what one wants it to do, rather than it going its own way, as it were. One's mind is experienced as much more supple and flexible, and at the same time, stable, much less distractible, even undistractible. Furthermore, the contents of one's consciousness become clearer, more vivid, and more differentiated.

Thinking about that, and what the Buddha would have been experiencing in comparison to those early psychologists of a hundred years ago, it became evident to me that the Buddha would have been, in a way, doing something similar to them, exploring the contents of consciousness, but because of the conditions he was in, and what precisely he was doing, he would have been much more successful in that exploration, and also in coming to understand the nature of consciousness. Also, the Buddha would have not only been in access concentration, he would be developing deeper levels of concentration, called the dhyanas, and also developing what Buddhists term 'insight', which is a clear, unbiased appreciation of crucial aspects of the nature of existence, in particular of mental states. In effect he would be exploring the structure and nature of consciousness to a far greater depth, with far greater rigour, than those psychologists of a hundred years ago.

An analogy came to me, that if one compares those psychologists with the Buddha, and what they were doing with what he was doing, it is rather like comparing an A level physics experiment at a local school with an experiment at the Large Hadron Collider at CERN. It is as far apart in complexity and depth of experience as that.

Now Titchener and his followers took what they were doing very seriously, and it is perhaps a sensible way to start if one is thinking of exploring human consciousness in a methodical way. The problem is, in comparison to the explorations of a successful meditator, this approach is likely to discover little.

Moreover there is also the background of physicalism, and the materialism that often goes along with it, and how that affected psychology. The question is – how was an early psychologist going to understand the existence of consciousness? Were they all like Titchener, accepting its existence and wishing to explore its features, although explaining it away as the functioning of the nervous system, or were some going to have other ideas, especially as strict materialism denies that consciousness exists at all?

What actually arose in the early twentieth century and replaced the work of Titchener and his followers, and of those German psychologists and the like, was behaviourism, which I mentioned briefly in the previous chapter.

Behaviourism is an approach to the study of human psychology which rules out of consideration any discussion of the contents of consciousness. Discussion about consciousness, from a behaviourist point of view, is being unscientific. According to behaviourists, the most one is able to be, in discussing consciousness, is very subjective, but one is probably just mistaken. Instead one should just study human behaviour, which can be observed and measured.

Behaviourism arose particularly from the ideas of an American called John Watson. It was a new movement in psychology replacing those earlier developments. Behaviourism arose and emphasised that all one can study is the observable *behaviour* of human beings, and do that in ways rather like one can study the behaviour of animals. As I mentioned in my last chapter, behaviourism developed into the study of rats in cages being rewarded for pressing levers. Behaviourists seemed to believe that that was the path to understanding human psychology. Behavioural psychology became a study of the 'conditioning' of patterns of behaviour through schedules of 'reinforcement' (3).

Behaviourism became very influential, and more or less the dominant form of psychology, as academic psychology grew in the twentieth century. It arose from physicalist and materialist assumptions, and it was probably a manifestation of the most extreme version of such philosophy, ruling out the existence of consciousness, more or less at all. For the most part, behaviourists were strict materialists.

If one looks at materialists who deny the existence of consciousness they are often inconsistent. Sometimes they deny consciousness exists at all, and at other times they say, in effect, that it exists but is not really anything other than the activity of the nervous system – with various attempted explanations given as to how that is so. Thus there is a spectrum of materialist positions with regard to consciousness, from complete denial of existence, through an inconsistent acceptance of its existence, to a full acceptance but nevertheless believing it to be a material phenomenon. This spectrum was there in the early discipline of psychology. However behaviourism, with a strict denial of consciousness, came to dominate.

If we consider the earlier schools of scientific psychology they also appear to have been very narrow in focus, both on the contents of consciousness and also how they related to physical stimuli. Behaviourism then focused upon rats in cages. But what about what one might call psychology in the real world? What about, for example, the study and treatment of the psychological problems that people have, including mental health problems?

At the end of the nineteenth century there began to be developments of what one would now call psychotherapy. This was not due to psychologists. Psychology was an academic discipline practised by relatively few people, and it had not long been in existence. But there were members of another profession who were having to deal with real people, in the real world, and their problems, especially their mental health problems. Those people were doctors, primarily neurologists and psychiatrists. At the end of the nineteenth century various neurologists and psychiatrists were developing what one could call the first forms of psychotherapy.

So, for example, in Paris there were neurologists like Jean-Martin Charcot and Pierre Janet, based at the Salpetriere mental hospital, and treating certain mental health problems using psychological techniques (4). Also, in the German world, psychological therapies were beginning to be developed and taken seriously. These doctors treated things like the psychological effects of trauma. They also studied what was apparently a common condition in those days, called 'hysteria'. In the late nineteenth century there seemed to be many people suffering from hysteria. This condition consisted of attacks of psychological and physical symptoms that appeared to have no physical explanation. Doctors such as Charcot and Janet started specialising in hysteria and studying what might be the causes of it. What they realised was that the causes were psychological.

Charcot and Janet also realised that, with regard to hysteria, one had to take into account that the people suffering from this were, as they put it, suffering from 'ideas' that were 'unconscious' – that they had some idea or other, and somehow had suppressed the idea, or memory of it, but the idea, which was typically a very distressing one, was still having an effect on their mental state and behaviour.

For example, Pierre Janet gave a detailed exposition of a case of a young woman who every month had an attack of hysteria, with physical and psychological symptoms. He gradually managed to work out, from her accounts of when that started, that it began with her first menstruation, which had frightened her very much. She had thought something was very wrong with her and attempted to stop it happening, and had got very frightened by it. But when he first talked to her, when she became his patient, she had had no apparent memory of this. She had also experienced other distressing events which she had forgotten and which seemed to be related to her hysterical symptoms.

So doctors like Charcot and Janet were thinking in terms of there being unconscious processes in the human mind which adversely affected people's mental state and behaviour. The theory that there are 'unconscious' processes affecting human psychology had actually been growing through the nineteenth century. The philosopher Johan Herbart had hypothesised the existence of unconscious ideas, and considered that each such idea possessed a certain active force, with mental life being a struggle between ideas. Charcot and Janet were, in effect, using similar theories to Herbart in their work.

At the end of the nineteenth century, however, there came Sigmund Freud. He was an Austrian doctor who studied under Charcot and who undertook the psychological treatment of people himself, including many people with hysteria. Freud is often believed to have started the idea of there being 'unconscious' psychological processes, and even with starting psychotherapy. Neither belief is correct.

Now Freud, as I mentioned in my last essay, was strongly influenced by the theories of physics at the time – theories which were concerned with energy, and the conservation of energy. Freud developed his therapy, which came to be called psychoanalysis, by thinking about the human mind in terms of an energy, a physical type of energy, that was conserved. His theories of unconscious functioning were based upon such ideas about energy (5).

If one thinks of classical psychoanalytic treatment it is of a patient lying on a couch saying whatever comes into their mind, and every now and again the psychoanalyst might make a comment. When the psychoanalyst is making a comment, they are giving an 'interpretation' of what the patient has been saying or doing, making that interpretation based upon Freudian theory – the belief being that making such interpretations helps the person overcome whatever problem they suffer. Whether this worked is very questionable.

So whilst behaviourism was developing and becoming dominant in psychology, psychoanalysis was developing and coming to dominate in the world of psychotherapy. It is sobering to consider that during the first half of the twentieth century the main forms of thinking in the West about human psychology were behaviourism, which did not recognise the existence of consciousness, and psychoanalysis, which considered that hypothetical unconscious processes, based upon physical energy, were most important.

Psychoanalysis also became very influential within society as a whole. Freud became famous and was taken very seriously. So by the mid-twentieth century Freud was being taken by many as one of the most important scientists that there has been, with the belief that he had made fundamental discoveries about human psychology, based on 'scientific' theories, and that these discoveries were highly important. As one professor wrote:

"Thanks to Freud's singular genius, he was to discover... that the laws of dynamics could be applied to man's personality as well as to his body. When he made his discovery Freud proceeded to create a dynamic psychology. A dynamic psychology is one that studies the transformations and exchanges of energy within the personality. This was Freud's greatest achievement, and one of the greatest achievements in modern science. It is certainly the crucial event in the history of psychology." (6)

It was also widely believed that if one did psychotherapy it really needed to be psychoanalysis. Nevertheless, other forms of psychotherapy had been developing. There was Jung, another psychiatrist at the end of the nineteenth century, who also became interested in unconscious processes. He worked with Freud for a while, but then parted company. Jung is noteworthy because he had a very different take on human beings to the materialists. Jung became interested in myth, symbol and religion. Given the dominant trends, of physicalism and its expression in behaviourism and psychoanalysis, Jung was very much an exception in the first part of the twentieth century. However, by the 1960s and 1970s Jungian therapy was becoming more widespread, and more widely known.

There were other developments in therapy. Carl Rogers developed 'client centred counselling', which he contrasted with psychoanalysis. Rogers believed that the basis of his counselling is that if a person with a psychological problem has somebody to talk to, the counsellor, who is warm, genuine, empathic, non-directive and non-judgmental, then that in itself can bring about change. Rogers was very confident that a positive relationship with the counsellor could itself bring about change.

There also developed the 'experiential' therapies, which emphasised the deliberate experience, within the therapy situation, of emotions connected with psychological problems. Gestalt therapy is perhaps the most notable of these.

Then, by the 1960s and 1970s there were beginning to be new influences on psychology and psychotherapy. Clinical psychologists were beginning to be more in evidence, although there were still not very many of them, but more than there used to be. Such clinical psychologists often developed and practised behaviour therapy, stemming from behaviourism. Behaviour therapy itself was a very practical approach to mental health problems, a practical approach that was missing in psychoanalysis, counselling and most other forms of therapy. The behaviourist emphasis on 'reinforcement' and 'conditioning' contributed directly to this. This emphasis led to the analysis of the relationships between factors which perpetuated psychological problems. Such an analysis was later termed 'formulation'.

Psychologists, especially behaviour therapists, became very critical of psychoanalysis. They criticised it as being completely unscientific. In contrast, research into the actual effects of therapeutic interventions was championed by psychologists and behaviour therapists. Thus psychoanalysis and its dominant position in therapy came under attack, and by the 1960s and 1970s therapy was beginning to change. Freud was questioned very critically, and was not being taken nearly so seriously, and was even being ridiculed. There were also people who had tried psychoanalysis, who had trained in it, but who became disillusioned with it.

There was Aaron Beck, an American psychiatrist, who became interested in the treatment of depression, and who rejected psychoanalytic treatment for it. He developed what became known as cognitive therapy (7). Beck realised that when people are depressed they have certain types of thoughts which reinforce their depressed state. So he developed therapy around helping them see through the illogicalities of such thoughts – the thoughts being typically very illogical, and poorly related to evidence. Such an approach undermines the vicious circle of depressed mood and negative thoughts mutually reinforcing one another.

Beck was not the only person to realise the importance of thinking in psychological problems. There was another therapist called Albert Ellis, who earlier developed a similar therapy to cognitive therapy, called Rational Emotive Therapy. However it was Beck's cognitive therapy which became more influential.

Behaviour therapy was also beginning to bring practical methods to help people change, and to understand their psychological problems. This was an important shift – away from interpretation without practical advice, and away from non-directive counselling. There is a certain irony to behaviour therapy, because to help people practically with their psychological problems one has to take seriously their conscious experience, which behaviourism strictly denied. However, in the 1980s, partly under the influence of the rise of cognitive therapy, behaviour therapy developed into cognitive behaviour therapy, which then became the dominant form of therapy.

Meanwhile, in psychology, behaviourism itself had been fading. What happened in the 1950s and 1960s was the development of computers, and people started to consider the human mind, and human thinking, in comparison to computer functioning. That made people realise that perhaps one should take into account at least what people think when one is trying to understand human psychology.

So by the mid-1970s, which is when I was an undergraduate in psychology, the earlier twentieth century psychology and therapy were changing. Although in my undergraduate courses in psychology there was still quite a behavioural emphasis, there were other approaches in them besides behaviourism. One could study quite a few different viewpoints on psychology. When doing my undergraduate degree I decided that behaviourism really was foolish, and also in reading up on Freud and psychoanalysis concluded that psychoanalysis was in large part wrong as well. I did not realise at the time where the thinking underlying behaviourism and psychoanalysis had come from – what I now term physicalism. But as an undergraduate at the time, I was not impressed. I wanted to do clinical psychology and understand people, and these two approaches did not seem to be right at all. There was however one aspect of the later psychoanalytic tradition, called 'object relations', which I found useful. This involved the recognition that people's behaviour and mental states tended to be strongly influenced by internalised models of the relationships they had experienced as children. This observation complemented what research into 'attachment theory' was reporting. I also found Jung's exploration of myth and symbol very helpful, although I now disagree strongly with his theories (about 'individuation' and 'archetypes').

Around that time in the 1970s, in psychotherapy there were other influences coming in as well, in particular influences from the East. This is the time of the hippies, and influences on the West from India, particularly Hindu thought, and from China and the Far East, such as Taoism. Tai Chi was beginning to be taught in the West then, and yoga was becoming popular. What was also coming in and starting to influence people's thinking was Buddhism, particularly Zen Buddhism. For whatever historical reasons, Zen became much more widely known than other types of Buddhism at that time.

By the 1960s books started to appear comparing Eastern spiritual traditions, including Buddhism, with psychology and psychotherapy, for example, Alan Watts' 'Psychotherapy East and West' (8). In 1960 there was published a book called 'Zen Buddhism and Psychoanalysis', by Fromm, Suzuki and De Martino, looking at similarities and differences between Zen Buddhism and psychoanalysis (9). Around that time another book came out, by a Sinhalese scholar, Padmasiri Da Silva, about Buddhism and psychoanalysis, comparing and contrasting the two – this time the Buddhism of the Pali Canon – and looking, for example, at ancient Buddhist ideas about unconscious processes (10).

Thus what was arising in the 1970s was a range of influences, with major changes occurring in the psychology and psychotherapy worlds, which were beginning to open up and become rather different, as they began to be affected by traditions other than that of the nineteenth century physicalist viewpoint. In particular, Buddhism was becoming more widely known. Originally, Buddhism became known in the West in the later nineteenth century, when people became very interested in it. Sir Edwin Arnold's poem, 'The Light of Asia', about the life of the Buddha, was written in 1879, and enjoyed a wide readership, and strongly affected people. For a while at least Buddhism was beginning to be taken seriously (11). But that interest seems to have faded, although it did result in some westerners becoming Buddhist monks at the beginning of the twentieth century.

By the 1970s what was also happening was the influence of westerners who had gone to the East and become Buddhists, whose thinking was now spreading back to the West. For me one of the very important influences was the German Buddhist, Lama Govinda, whose book 'Foundations of Tibetan Mysticism' made me realise I was a Buddhist. I had been well prepared for that book by reading Jung, which led to me being responsive to symbols and mythology, and therefore made it an easy and valuable book to read (12).

So there were western Buddhist practitioners like Lama Govinda, and also Sangharakshita, who was back in the West and beginning to teach and found a movement. Tibetan Buddhism was also becoming known in the West, with Tibetan practitioners moving here, especially after the Chinese takeover of Tibet and the persecution that that entailed. More generally, one could say that in the late 1970s the West was a cultural melting pot. In this context some people were taking the idea seriously that Buddhist practices could help in psychotherapy. This meant that in the 1970s, and through into the 1980s, various people, not necessarily known to each other, began to use aspects of Buddhist practice within therapy.

For example, Ron Kurtz developed Hakomi Therapy, starting in the 1970s. Hakomi Therapy is based upon mindfulness (13). In England at the beginning of the 1980s Maura Sills and her husband Franklyn developed Core Process Psychotherapy, also based upon mindfulness (14). Thus these people were beginning to develop forms of therapy based on Buddhist ideas and practices. There were also people like myself, not necessarily developing specific forms of therapy but using aspects of Buddhist practice within the therapy we were doing. I myself was using mindfulness and metta bhavana within therapy.

Gradually what developed in the 1980s were the beginnings of a network of people in the psychotherapy and psychology worlds who were taking practices like mindfulness seriously. I mentioned Hakomi and Core Process Psychotherapy, but the two specific forms of therapy based upon mindfulness that began to be taken much more seriously in the world of therapy and psychology were developed by another two people, in America.

The first was developed by John Kabat-Zinn, who devised a form of therapy for pain management based upon mindfulness. This later became known as Mindfulness Based Stress Reduction (15). He was doing that in Boston, and started in the 1970s. I came across some published research by him in the late 1980s, and was interested that someone was using mindfulness and doing research on it. In the world of psychology and mainstream therapy, research is important. Forms of therapy have to be backed by research showing they are effective. (Many types of therapy have been developed without this. So, however effective they might be, they did not necessarily get taken seriously within the world of mainstream psychology and therapy.)

Meanwhile, on the other side of America, in Seattle, Marsha Linehan was developing a form of therapy for people with emotionally unstable personality disorder (otherwise known as borderline personality disorder) (16). These are people who experience very extreme emotions, such as anger, and who self-harm, and often create major scenes. They are people who can be really difficult to treat.

Marsha Linehan developed a form of therapy specifically for them, based upon mindfulness training, called Dialectical Behaviour Therapy. Through the 1990s this came to be widely known about, and was taken very seriously. Up to that point nobody had had any effective therapy for borderline personality disorder. Suddenly somebody was coming up with something, backed up by some research.

So by the 1990s the therapy world was becoming more interested in, and taking more seriously, a specific Buddhist practice. This interest was increased when a particular group of researchers started to take mindfulness training seriously themselves, and developed a form of therapy for depression, called Mindfulness Based Cognitive Therapy. That group of researchers was John Teasdale and his associates. They had been studying depression and its treatment.

I remember talking with a clinical psychologist who was one of John Teasdale's research assistants in the late 1980s, who told me that they had come to realise that how, what Buddhists would say, 'mindful' someone is, is an important predictor of how effective cognitive therapy would be. So they came to the conclusion that therapy needed some form of mindfulness training. They eventually developed Mindfulness Based Cognitive Therapy after exploring Jon

Kabat-Zinn's mindfulness based therapy (17). This in turn led to increased interest in mindfulness as a therapy intervention. Meanwhile, others had also been developing mindfulness related therapies, such as Acceptance and Commitment Therapy. Thus by the early years of this century Buddhist ideas were becoming even more influential in the world of therapy.

Nowadays one can hardly pick up a psychology journal without seeing the word 'mindfulness' in one or other of the articles in it. There is even an academic journal called 'Mindfulness'. The therapies based on mindfulness have been given the label 'third wave therapies'. There are a variety of different therapeutic approaches nowadays based around mindfulness, and one can go on academic courses about it. Through the world of psychology and psychotherapy 'mindfulness' is everywhere. It has also spread to education and business.

Also what has happened in the last ten years or so is not just the use of mindfulness in therapy, but much academic study of the effectiveness of mindfulness therapy. There has also been the rise of neuroscience research on what happens when people are meditating. So there has been an increasing number of studies looking at, for example, people who are doing basic mindfulness courses, eight week courses, and at what happens to their brains through doing the course. What they are finding is that after an eight-week course there are demonstrable changes in the functioning and structure of people's brains – that is in just eight weeks (18).

Alongside that, there have been neurological studies of meditators, mainly Tibetan (the Dalai Lama having encouraged such study), people who have been meditating a long time. These studies have been finding indeed that such experienced meditators have brains that are functioning rather differently to the average person's brain. For example, if one looks at Tibetan monks who have been doing lots of meditation on compassion, what one finds is that those parts of the brain, that we now know are associated with feeling happy, and also with feeling empathic towards others, are very well developed (19).

Perhaps this is not really surprising. What neuroscience has been discovering is that the brain, the functioning and structure of the brain, changes depending upon what one does. Therefore meditation affects it.

There seems to be much continuing interest in the neuroscience of meditation. Indeed, there is another academic journal that I came across called the Journal of Neuroscience, Consciousness and Spirituality.

Looking at the last thirty years or so, I would say that the important developments in psychology and psychotherapy have been the 'cognitive revolution' (based in part on the development of computers, and in part on the rise of cognitive therapy), and the development of behaviour therapy which then became cognitive behaviour therapy, the dominant form of therapy within the orthodox medical/psychological world. Cognitive behaviour therapy has a strong emphasis on teaching people skills, and teaching them how to understand their own mind. This is markedly different to psychoanalysis and Rogerian counselling.

Cognitive behaviour therapy dovetails very well with mindfulness based and other Buddhist approaches. Interestingly, there is an essay from the 1980s by a psychologist at the Maudsley in London, Padmal Da Silva, looking at behaviour therapy, and how various behaviour therapy techniques were in effect used within early Buddhism (20). He describes the Buddha, in effect, doing therapy with King Pasenadi, who was overweight through eating far too much. Da Silva quotes a passage from a Buddhist text detailing how the Buddha helped King Pasenadi to lose weight. The Buddha asked one of the princes to recite to the king a verse, just as he was about to eat the last mouthful of food at a meal. The verse was about not eating any more. That would stop the king taking the last mouthful. At the next meal the king was to be served only as much as he ate the last time, with the verse again being recited just before he took the last mouthful of this meal. So gradually, step by step, the king was eating less and less - a structured approach to losing weight, not a sudden crash diet.

Over the last thirty years mainstream psychological therapy has been dominated by cognitive behaviour therapy, with Buddhist methods coming in increasingly, and with the consequent development of what have now been called the 'third wave' therapies. Nevertheless there is another branch of psychological study that deserves mention. This is attachment theory. In my second essay I mentioned the issue of attachment, in relation to the Buddha encouraging the cultivation of a love for others closely akin to maternal love. What has developed over the last sixty years has been the study of childhood attachments, their problems, and how those problems affect psychological functioning and mental health in childhood and adulthood. In my work as a psychologist, and as a Buddhist aware of the issues that inhibit people's engagement with Buddhist practice, particularly with developing deep friendships, I have become very aware how problematic attachments developing in childhood (usually due to abuse or neglect) can lead to major psychological difficulties.

So, not only do I consider attachment to be a central aspect of being human, but I also consider that attachment problems are major inhibitors of both psychological and spiritual health. Attachment theory, and those therapies specifically including methods to overcome attachment related problems, can be useful means to help people develop psychological health, and in particular can be helpful to the practising Buddhist who has attachment problems to overcome (21).

Apart from attachment problems, another important issue is that of the effects of trauma upon psychological health, and the western psychological study and treatment of such effects. There is also the understanding of, and treatments for, mental health problems and psychological difficulties generally, within western psychology and psychotherapy. All such accurate knowledge and effective practice can of course be helpful to the Buddhist as much as to other people. They complement a specifically Buddhist approach, which focuses more upon moral issues within psychology, by bringing in understanding of other aspects of psychological conditioning which traditional Buddhism has not usually explicitly considered.

Generally, with regard to the application of Buddhist ideas and practices within psychological therapy, to me it seems that this is a very positive development. Increasing numbers of people can make use of Buddhist practices to improve their mental health. One does not need to be a Buddhist to do the practices. Buddhist practices are means for human beings to develop their psychological qualities and skills. So it is good to see these practices spreading, so that many people can get the benefits of them. Perhaps, too, the interplay between Buddhism and psychological therapy is not surprising. Once psychology and therapy had begun to overcome their physicalist and materialist origins, and with Buddhism becoming known in the west, it is natural to compare the two, and consider what each has to offer the other. Both are concerned with psychological analysis and positive psychological development.

It is also good, from a Buddhist point of view, that Buddhist practices are getting widely known, because it raises the profile of Buddhism in the world. My perception over the last thirty years is that Buddhism does not tend to make it into serious debate in the West. It is sidelined and not taken seriously, and usually simply misunderstood. I suspect that the developments now, with respect to mindfulness, mean Buddhism is actually, at least in certain areas, entering the mainstream. Perhaps through its spread into the world of psychology it might become more generally known and properly understood in the wider world, and the restricted choice of 'god or nothing' overcome.

With regard to that restricted choice, the influence of Buddhism upon psychology may prove beneficial in fully overcoming the physicalist and materialist assumptions upon which psychology was started. This might also help undermine materialist assumptions in the world at large, and help with the realisation that one can be scientific without being either materialist or physicalist.

However, one concern I have as a Buddhist is that the spread of Buddhist practices in therapy might be accompanied by serious misunderstandings of Buddhist ideas. For example, there is the question of the interpretations of 'mindfulness' that psychologists and therapists are using. I will quote from John Kabat-Zinn. He defined mindfulness as "paying attention in a particular way: on purpose, in the present moment, and non-judgmentally". John Teasdale and his colleagues use this definition too.

Now 'mindfulness' is a translation of '*sati*' which originally literally meant 'memory', although in Buddhist practice it came to mean more than that. There is an aspect of mindfulness which is about continuity of purpose, or memory of what you are meant to be doing, keeping continuously to your intended actions. Traditionally this has gone alongside being aware of current experience, as the two fundamental aspects of mindfulness. Kabat-Zinn's definition mentions paying attention "on purpose". However in western therapists' understanding of mindfulness there is typically a strong emphasis on awareness of the present moment, as well as being 'non-judgmental'.

The emphasis on awareness of the present moment and being non-judgmental needs to be unpacked somewhat. I particularly thought that after coming across an article in the Scientific American's psychology magazine where a psychologist was going into Broadmoor hospital looking at the supposed mindfulness of psychopaths (22). The issue is that psychopaths focus on what happens now and downplay what is going to happen in the future. To talk about what psychopaths do as mindfulness seems to me to be completely missing the point. Crucially there is the whole question of continuity of intention, which underlies paying attention – the 'purpose' aspect of mindfulness. From a Buddhist perspective mindfulness, as awareness of present experience, is accompanied by continuity of intention, of purpose. This has to be an ethical purpose. That brings to the fore the whole question of something that has been missing from psychology and therapy – the question of morality. In Buddhism there is the threefold path of sila, samadhi, prajna. One could say of these terms that sila means moral integrity, samadhi means psychological integration, and prajna means wisdom.

In contrast, Western psychology has not really taken morality into consideration at all. That is not the fault of psychology itself, because in the West the problem has been what is left of the philosophy of morality if one gets beyond the idea of a ruling, creator god – typically one gets moral relativism. So there is not a basis upon which psychologists may build in considering morality and its importance for human psychological health. From a Buddhist perspective morality is crucial. Within Buddhism it is recognised that the moral nature of the motivation behind one's actions influences one's psychological integration, one's level of happiness, and the state of one's mind (and of course affects other people). One could put it that moral integrity is a factor in the development of psychological integration, and vice versa.

The fact that morality is missing is a factor of major importance in assessing the western understanding of psychology. Its lack is also likely to affect how westerners understand mindfulness, particularly in how they understand being 'non-judgmental'. Actually, on a practical level, learning to be 'non-judgmental' can be very important, because people who are depressed, for example, are often very self-critical, very hard on themselves, and for them, and for many other people with mental health problems, it is very important to get out of the automatic habit of putting oneself down – being non-judgmental in this way is thus a healthy development. But being 'non-judgmental', especially when combined with attending to the present moment, can be wrongly taken to imply an amoral or even immoral attitude, unconcerned about the future consequences of one's actions, as with psychopaths.

Furthermore, in the western interpretation of mindfulness there does not seem to be any clear understanding, as far as I can gather, of more concentrated states of mind. Earlier I mentioned access concentration and dhyana. So far these do not seem to have been taken seriously within the psychology and therapy worlds (except perhaps with regard to the neuroscience of meditation).

There may be various reasons for that, but I remember a discussion I had with other psychologists and people interested in Buddhism and therapy at a seminar in the 1980s. It was very clear that I was the only one there who took seriously the importance of mental states like access concentration and dhyana. For the others there, talking about such mental states was somehow wrong. The fact that it was in the Buddhist tradition seemed to be downplayed or ignored. There seemed to be an assumption that to consider more concentrated mental states as in some way better was being inegalitarian. I think there were also influences from specific Buddhist traditions, such as Chan (Zen). Thich Nhat Hanh (from the Vietnamese Chan tradition) criticises the cultivation of dhyana and even argues that its cultivation is not a Buddhist practice (23). (This is ironic as the terms Chan and Zen are the Chinese and Japanese pronunciations of 'dhyana'.) I strongly disagree with him.

So in the West, at least in the eighties, there was the idea around that somehow to get into more deeply concentrated states of consciousness in meditation is somehow elitist and wrong. I do wonder how much that sort of thinking is behind interpretations of mindfulness that are now circulating in the world of therapy and psychology. This is because such thinking is associated with a conception of 'tolerance' which amounts to accepting different views as equal, and believing that one should not criticise or judge them. Emphasising being 'non-judgmental' within mindfulness practice then seems to parallel such beliefs.

Looking ahead, I wonder what developments there are going to be, within psychology and psychotherapy, given the Buddhist influence. More generally, as I mentioned in my last chapter, perhaps we are at the edge of a major change in how the world is understood. I have discussed the physicalism of the nineteenth century, and the development of materialist views contrasting with a theistic cultural background. Such thinking became dominant and has lasted into this century, being still with us in many ways. It replaced the old Catholic view, combined with Aristotle, of a thousand years ago, which was the dominant view for centuries. So I wonder if we are on the edge of a major shift again, with people exploring consciousness - maybe taking consciousness seriously and not just trying to explain it away as being nothing but physical matter, with at the same time Buddhist practices coming in, and interfacing very well with modern psychology and therapy, and with modern neuroscience. I hope that a growing understanding of natural ethics becomes an integral part of such a shift. I find this situation exciting, although I also do wonder whether the development of 'secular Buddhism' – i.e. a materialist interpretation of Buddhism – might inhibit this paradigm change.

Hopefully, too, Buddhist ideas will spread to other areas of mainstream thought, such as the philosophy of ethics. Or consider sociology, a subject much limited by political beliefs stemming from physicalism. I started to think about sociology in relation to the old Buddhist symbol of the 'wheel of life'. If one thinks about the realms of the wheel of life, and does not take them literally, what they are in essence depicting are different cultures and subcultures, and the behaviour and mental states that predominate in those cultures and subcultures. The Buddhist emphasis is on the ethical nature of the motivations underlying the actions, which may perpetuate specific cultures and subcultures – particular dominant patterns of motivation, mental state and behaviour persisting and reinforcing each other. I suspect that to analyse cultures and subcultures in this way would be very fruitful.

For example, one could analyse the world of stockbroking in this way, or an inner-city teenage gang. Such an analysis of what one could call the 'moral patterning' of cultures and subcultures could be a part of a wider analysis looking at the overall patterns of conditionality within them. The interaction between culture and attachment patterns would also be important when trying to understand the healthiness of human cultures. I consider that an important question to ask, with respect to any particular culture or subculture, is how much it encourages and helps the development of positive attachments in childhood, or whether, on the contrary, it undermines such development. More generally one could investigate the interaction between cultures, mental health, attachment and morality.

7

Buddhism, Complexity and Modern Physics

I have discussed previously how ideas based upon classical Newtonian physics were misapplied to human behaviour and the human world. In this chapter I am first going to look at an area of modern science, called complexity theory, which gives a very different understanding of the human world to those earlier misapplied ideas. Then I will turn to modern physics, with regard to which I will be exploring the Buddhist principles of conditionality and emptiness. I will look in particular at what those principles would imply, if we interpret them in a way that applies to physics, and how that compares to modern theories of physics. There are some very interesting parallels. These relate to some central aspects of modern theories of physics, which give a markedly different perspective on the physical world itself, contrasting with the theories of classical physics.

First, I will recapitulate what conditionality is about: the term 'conditionality' refers to *pratitya samutpada*. This Sanskrit term has various translations: conditioned co-production; interdependent arising, inter-related conditionality, or conditionality (for short). Pratitya samutpada is a principle. It points to an understanding of the world that actually cannot be put into words, but one can take it as an expression in words, in ideas, pointing to the nature of reality.

When it was originally used, by the Buddha himself, he applied it to human life, and how people either get caught in endless cycles of repetitive mental states and behaviour, or else progress psychologically and spiritually. Moreover, if one reads descriptions in Buddhist texts of how the principle was applied by him, it was in a very pragmatic way. Using the principle of conditionality the Buddha described important aspects of people's behaviour and mental states, looking at how those different aspects conditioned each other. He was describing how different phenomena associated with human beings reinforce each other, so that, in a way, we go round and round in circles, stuck in the same old mental states and behaviour. Alternatively, we might progress out of those vicious circles and develop more ethical behaviour, more positive mental states, and deeper wisdom about the world, in a process to which the Buddha also applied the principle of conditionality (1).

I emphasise that pratitya samutpada is essentially a pragmatic formula, and there are instances in the old texts of the Buddha applying it in different ways, looking at how psychological and ethical phenomena condition each other. This is very reminiscent of 'formulation' in psychology, which I mentioned in my last chapter.

Formulation in psychology is a way of looking at factors in someone's life, that is phenomena in their mental states and in what they are doing, as well as in the world around them, that keep their mental health difficulties going. For example, if someone has a phobia, formulation involves looking at how that phobia is kept going, what factors maintain it in what one could call 'vicious circles' of feedback – in order to work out a practical way to stop the phobia happening. Formulation is not an exhaustive catalogue of all the factors affecting someone, but a pragmatic depiction of the important factors for the issues in question – how their suffering is maintained and what to do about that. Thus if we look at the phenomena that influence human beings, both internal and external to them, they are very many and highly complicated. However formulation looks at the crucial factors maintaining a specific psychological difficulty.

This is very similar to the application of *pratitya samutpada* by the Buddha. He identified certain important phenomena concerning human suffering and how it is maintained, and looked at how they conditioned each other.

However, we can also consider the term *pratitya samutpada* as a *general* principle of 'conditionality', and as not just applying to specific aspects of human life. We can ask how it might apply in other areas as well, such as the phenomena of physics. Does the principle of conditionality apply to the physical world, and if so, how?

Now if one thinks about the principle, as a general principle, then it becomes very clear that that is what it is – a very general principle. In considering this I realised that it is, as I have mentioned, a pragmatic principle, and if one attempts to apply it to the physical world, what it implies is that one must go and investigate the physical phenomena in question, exploring what exactly they are and how they condition each other - how, for example, with the arising of such and such a phenomenon, such as an electric force, another phenomenon, such as an electron, is affected.

From this perspective *pratitya samutpada* is in effect a principle, or an underlying rationale, for empirical study. One could say that it actually seems to be a rationale, an underlying principle, for scientific study. I would suggest that it is *the* underlying rationale for science.

So one can take *pratitya samutpada* to be a principle that one follows in order to find out more about the world, on whatever level. The Buddha himself applied it pragmatically to human beings and our spiritual life (or lack of it). But we can apply the same general formula to any area of evidence, any set of phenomena – but we have to do the work of finding out precisely what those phenomena are, and what exactly the relationships between them are. So, applied generally, the *pratitya samutpada* formula does not tell us very much, but looked at another way it is implying that we need to do empirical study – that we find out what the patterns of relatedness, patterns of conditionality, actually are.

One can also consider the principle of conditionality, and compare it and contrast it with ideas I have discussed before, in particular the idea of 'natural law' in the human world and the physical world. As I have emphasised, the idea that grew up in the West was that there were 'natural laws' underlying the world, underlying human psychology, underlying the physical world, underlying human action – and that what science was about was finding out what these natural laws are.

The principle of conditionality has similarities with the idea of natural law, if one thinks of a natural law as the explicit depiction of a specific pattern of conditionality. There are definite parallels. On the other hand there seems to be a difference. With *pratitya samutpada* there is no mention of 'law'. The concept of 'law' implies the existence of a law giver, and in the western context the law giver is supposed to be a ruling, creator god. Buddhism does not recognise such a god, so to talk of law with respect to *pratitya samupada* is somewhat misleading.

So *pratitya samupada* contrasts with the idea of natural law, first of all because there is no law giver. However, it also contrasts with it in another way as well. *Pratitya samutpada* is about conditionality, about there being conditions, and if one ponders the formula one can come to realise that it is not only implying that one actively finds out about phenomena, but also that there is a deeper implication. This deeper implication is that if the particular set of conditions one is studying and researching do not actually occur at times then things might be very different. This is a marked contrast to the idea of natural law, where there is believed to be one set law which everything obeys. It is more like there is conditionality and one can find out patterns of how phenomena inter-relate, but that is as far as one can go. Things might be different under other circumstances, other conditions.

So there is a more 'open' aspect to *pratitya samutpada*, compared to the idea of a 'natural law'. The *pratitya samutpada* formula implies that the conditions one is studying might not apply at times. Things might be rather different; the nature of reality is more 'open'. I am stressing this as an important implication of *pratitya samutpada* in contrast to the traditional western idea of natural law, where everything is considered to be under the same law. From the Buddhist point of view one can say 'maybe things could be different'.

In my earlier essays I discussed how people developed ideas about natural law taken from classical physics, and misapplied them to the human world. What is interesting and sad about how they applied them was that they were quite deterministic in how they thought human society would evolve, and by the nineteenth century very physicalist.

These days one does not have to be a Buddhist to come to recognise the problems of the nineteenth century physicalist way of trying to understand the human world. We have the advantage of computers now, and can study systems, interacting systems, by modelling them on computers. We can study systems far better than they could in the nineteenth century. Moreover there has developed a field of study called complexity theory, the study of complex interacting systems (2). Complexity theory has a very strong implication for ideas about the human world stemming from nineteenth century physics. Very simply, it shows them up as being based upon false and inapplicable assumptions.

Complex systems in the human world are systems where, with regard to the individual agents that make up the systems, their behaviour is determined by what they think other agents are going to do. So, very often, if one is going to do something, one has to consider what other people might do, in order to decide the best course of action. A classic example is called the El Farol Bar problem (3). The El Farol Bar was open Thursday evenings playing very good music, and it attracted a lot of people who really liked the music. The problem was that the El Farol Bar was relatively small. If one went there on a Thursday evening when there were not so many people there, and got in, one had a good time – one could sit comfortably and hear the music. When lots and lots of people go it is very crowded and one does not have such a good time. So the question is: it is early on a Thursday evening, does one go or not? One might know that on the previous couple of Thursdays it has been jam packed, so what does one do?

There is no ultimate logical best thing necessarily to do, because it depends on what other people are going to do. So one has to think 'what decisions are other people going to make?' Then one's strategy might be: 'if it was full the last couple of weeks then perhaps people will be frightened off, so there will be less people going, so I'll go'. But then one might think 'but other people might think the same thing as me, and they will therefore go as well, and it will actually get too crowded again.' Well, complexity theory studies all the sorts of strategies one can have, and which ones come out best in the end. It can be different strategies in different conditions, the point being that there is no logical best thing to do, and one simply does not know what other people are going to do.

The implication to take from this about human behaviour, and human society generally, is that in making decisions, or choosing to act in a particular way, often we are taking into account what other people might do. So for example, consider the Dutch tulip bulb bubble of the seventeenth century. People started buying tulip bulbs, and paying more and more for them – they bought them thinking the price was going to go up, that other people were going to pay more for them. So they bought them. The prices got absolutely extraordinary, but then one day at the market some bulbs did not get sold, and then the prices crashed (4).

Actually we make such assumptions all the time. One is given some money, or earns some money, and one expects other people to give the same value to the money as oneself. One does not expect to go down the shops and find suddenly that the money is worthless. Phenomena like the value of money emerge out of a system of human interactions, and involve implicit beliefs about what other people are going to do.

This aspect of complex systems has a very significant logical consequence – that such systems do not behave like deterministic physical systems, and one cannot make assumptions that the human world contains similar 'laws' to physical ones. In other words, those nineteenth century physicalist beliefs about the human world are fundamentally wrong, *on this basis alone*.

It is worth looking at this with regard to economics. Free market theory assumes that people make rational choices, based upon more or less perfect information, in order to maximise their 'utility', or at least their profit. Apart from the empirical fact that most people do not behave rationally in this way when buying or selling, it is also evident that people's economic behaviour is strongly influenced by what they believe other people are going to do, as in the Dutch tulip bulb bubble.

One important lesson from complexity theory is that systems can go to extremes, and that the likelihood that this can happen is much more than predicted by, for example, the physicalist assumptions embedded within neoclassical economic theory. In my third essay, I quoted Paul Krugman describing economists as believing that financial crises, such as the one that eventually happened, were impossible. Complexity theory shows they are all too possible.

Complexity theory demonstrates that one does not have to be a Buddhist to realise that nineteenth century physicalist ideas about the human world are fundamentally mistaken. Now the interesting thing is that in the world of physics itself, nineteenth century science, with its underlying assumptions, has been superseded. Thus much twentieth century and current thinking about the human world has been based upon assumptions drawn from an approach to physics which has been found inadequate with regard to the physical world itself. Let us then look at physics, and in particular at the main theories of physics.

Firstly, there is classical physics, based upon ideas and theories that come from Isaac Newton and his fellow thinkers. Classical physics can still be used quite successfully in everyday contexts, a lot of the time. It gives reasonably good answers for many things, and is much easier to use than relativity theory or quantum mechanics. But for the study of fundamental aspects of physics it is radically wrong.

Isaac Newton developed the 'laws of motion', as well as a theory of gravitation. Underlying his thinking, if one studies his original text (the Principia), is the belief that the things he was considering, physical 'quantities', had an 'absolute' existence (5). He talked of "absolute, true, and mathematical" quantities of time and space. So, for example, when he was considering the position of things in space, when using his laws of motion, he believed that there was such a thing as an absolute position of an object in space. Stemming from this he believed in an 'absolute motion' of an object through space. He contrasted absolute quantities with what he called "relative, apparent, and common" quantities, where one measures something, and these are the quantities one actually obtains. Newton realised one could not measure the absolute quantities, for example precisely where a planet was in space, but that what one actually measured are the relative quantities – how far that planet is from the Earth, or where it is in the sky as observed from one's position on earth. Nevertheless he considered that the absolute values of the quantities do exist, even if they could not be directly measured.

Before Newton people had realised that planets were travelling in orbits around the sun. But if one studies the position of the planets in the sky at night, sometimes some of them seem to be reversing their direction, travelling in a 'retrograde' direction. People realised that the 'going backwards' in the sky was just an apparent motion because of the motion of the Earth in relation to that planet, but that actually that planet was still going round the sun in the same direction.

So they had the idea that the real motion, in particular the real quantities of that motion, such as the velocity, might be different from the apparent ones. Newton was generalizing from this, in theorising about the absolute values for quantities, for example the absolute velocity of a planet going through space, or that there is a real absolute time that is the same everywhere.

This brings me on to the second aspect of Buddhist principles, the principle of *śunyata*, or 'emptiness'. *Śunyata* applied to any phenomenon, including a physical one, implies that that phenomenon has no intrinsic existence of its own, unrelated to anything else. So fundamental particles, and the atoms and molecules made from them, do not have any intrinsic existence. Nor does any physical quantity, such as the distance between two things in space, or the time between two events. The principle of *śunyata* implies this. To use Newton's terminology, it is saying that they do not have any absolute existence. Thus there is no absolute time at any place, no absolute distance between two things, nor absolute position in space.

Now Newton was saying the very opposite. He was stating that there really are phenomena such as absolute distances, absolute positions in space, absolute velocities, and absolute times. So there is an interesting contradiction here between the Buddhist principle of *śunyata*, and what Newton actually believed. The important issue is that Newton's belief in absolute quantities has been overturned by developments in physics, in particular by the theory of relativity and by quantum mechanics. These actually undermine that belief in there being absolute values of quantities. Let us look into this.

Einstein first discovered this. When he was quite young he had already learned the nineteenth century formulae, named Maxwell's equations, for electromagnetism, including light. Then he did a 'thought experiment' one day – he tried to imagine what a light wave would look like if one were going alongside it at the same speed. What Einstein realised was that Maxwell's equations of electromagnetism imply that if one is travelling along beside the light wave, at the same speed, then the light wave would cease to exist (6). Einstein found that a very interesting and significant puzzle. Why should light not exist if one is going along beside it at the same speed?

Some years later he worked out the implications of that little 'thought experiment'. These were revolutionary. Einstein realised that, for example, to talk about the 'time' in two different places is not straightforward (7). How does one tell the time? To do this one needs a clock next to one, and the ability to read the time on it. This involves looking at it, which depends upon light coming from the clock face to one's eyes. But how does one know what is exactly the same time on the moon, especially if one has not got a clock there?

Suppose one does somehow get a clock there. How does one know that that clock tells the same time, or even ticks at the same rate, as the clock next to one? In pondering this question Einstein realised that to talk about the 'same time' in different places involves making assumptions about the constancy of the speed of light. After all, one has to be able to see both clocks; in other words light has to come from both of them to wherever one is. Einstein thought about this and worked on it mathematically. He realised that one has to make a specific assumption about light taking the same time to travel in opposite directions between the two places. His mathematics then led to answers that simply contradicted Newton's ideas about absolute time and space. In particular Einstein discovered that the rate at which time passes is dependent upon the frame of reference one is using, and that people using different reference frames will observe the flow of time differently. He also discovered that the distance between two places also depends upon the frame of reference one uses, and that the same is true of other physical quantities, such as the velocity of an object.

So, for example, imagine that a group of astronauts is travelling into space in a spaceship, straight away from the Earth at a speed of nine tenths the speed of light. Imagine that the astronauts on the spaceship have got a clock with them, and that you have got a clock next to you, and that you can see what is going on in the spaceship, through some sort of video link.

Now they are going away from you at nine tenths the speed of light. You look and see what is going on in their spacecraft, and what you see is that they all seem to be talking, and walking, and doing things, somewhat slower than you, and funnily enough their clock is going slower than yours.

Meanwhile the astronauts in the spacecraft are doing exactly the same, looking over the video link at you and your clock. Now one might think that because you are seeing them slowed up, with their clock going slower than yours, then they must look at you and see that you are speeded up and your clock is going faster than theirs.

But that is not the case. They look at your clock and see that your clock is going slower than theirs, and that you are slowed down.

This seems very strange, if not completely contradictory. So is this result just apparent, just an effect, and actually the real rate of the clocks are different from those observed? Einstein's equations and theory give an unequivocal 'no' in answer to this question – it is not an apparent effect, not some sort of illusion, it is actually real. From your point of view, in your frame of reference here on Earth, the astronaut's clock is really going slower. In their frame of reference, your clock is really going slower. The point is that there is no absolute time, and no absolute rate of flow of time. The rate at which time passes depends upon one's frame of reference.

In general, in Einstein's Special Theory of Relativity he was looking at frames of reference that travel at constant velocities in relation to each other, called 'inertial frames'. If people are in different inertial frames of reference and they measure something then they will get different results, and everybody will be correct, yet all those results differ because there are no absolute values to the quantities of space and time, velocity, or physical quantities that derive from them.

In other words, phenomena such as time, space, distance and velocity have no intrinsic existence, to use Buddhist terminology. Their existence depends upon the relationship between the person measuring them and those physical things they are trying to measure.

It is not usually put like this. However, the lack of 'absolute' quantities is a very interesting and close parallel with the Buddhist concept of the lack of inherent existence. Einstein also went on to develop the General Theory of Relativity, in which it became even more clear that in different frames of reference the values of what one measures are different. Moreover Einstein's General Theory shows that space and time can be 'bent' or 'curved', and this is an explanation of the force of gravity.

What is quite striking is that the 'frame dependence' of the values of quantities – i.e. that quantities are actually different for different frames of reference – goes along with what Einstein calls the 'principle of relativity'. This principle is that physical laws are the same for everybody. So the mathematics, of how one writes down the physical laws, applies to everybody, and there is the same general physical truth in different frames of reference. However the measurements everyone gets are different, and everybody is correct (8). (The 'principle of relativity' is somewhat misleadingly named, as it is a theory that there are *general* truths, i.e. truths the same for everyone, as expressed in mathematical equations about the motion of objects. These general truths go along with the frame dependence of the quantities measured, quantities whose inter-relationships are expressed in those generally true mathematical formulae.)

This tends to defy our usual way of thinking about the world, for example that that there must be a specific distance between two objects. Suppose that I measure the distance between opposite walls of my study as being three metres. Well, that is true in my frame of reference here on earth, but if one were travelling in that spaceship at about nine tenths the speed of light, one would find that the distance was a bit less than three metres. If one were travelling even faster than that, even nearer the speed of light, one might find the walls are just a centimetre apart, and that would be equally true.

Thus there is not any inherent value to the quantity that is 'the' distance between myself and my study window. This is true of any physical quantities, according to the Theory of Relativity. One could say that, in the appropriate rest frame, quantities have specific values, but that is in the rest frame. In other frames of reference the values of those quantities are not the same. These are real differences, not just apparent ones.

Now our usual way of thinking about the world is that phenomena have an intrinsic existence - that a chair, for example, has an inherent existence, whether or not we are observing or measuring it, no matter what speed we are going at, and that that intrinsic existence implies it has intrinsic attributes that are there as aspects of the chair, and as this is a physical object we can measure them, and specify its intrinsic length and intrinsic height, and so on. But relativity theory is telling us that, actually, this is not the case.

It is hard to grasp the implications of this. What is interesting about studying modern physics is that people can do the mathematics, or at least some people can do the mathematics, but even the people who can do that do not necessarily understand the implications of what they are using, that is the philosophical implications for how we understand the world. (The mathematics does their thinking for them, one could say.) But actually it is very interesting to consider, with regard to relativity, the implications for one's ordinary assumptions,

assumptions like there is a specific distance between myself and my window, or that I have a particular height. Relativity theory shows it is not as simple as that.

In relativity theory, however, there are still assumptions, and those assumptions are that in any particular frame of reference, for example the rest frame, that when you are not measuring something the quantity you would be measuring is still there in some way. For example, such an assumption would be that I am six foot in height and if no-one is looking at me, or measuring me, I am still six feet high in my frame of reference. (I might be three feet high in another frame of reference.) This assumption seems very reasonable.

So there is still an assumption in relativity theory that the values of quantities exist, even when one is not measuring them, and that they somehow have some independence from the process of measurement. Now is that true of the physical world in general? Is it true, for example, with respect to the 'fundamental particles' that make up our bodies and the world around us - the electrons, protons and such like. Do those things have attributes to which one can find specific values, and which actually exist, without measuring them?

Consider an electron. If one is not looking at it, not measuring it in some way, does it have a specific location in space, at least in one's own frame of reference? Does it have a specific velocity? Classical physics would say most definitely yes, and even relativity theory implies that, in a given frame of reference, it definitely has specific quantities and definitely exists in a specific place at a given time, with a definite velocity.

The interesting thing is that another branch of modern physics, Quantum Mechanics, makes it quite clear that particles such as electrons do not have such an intrinsic existence when one is not measuring them (or at least when they are not interacting with other particles). The classic procedure demonstrating this is called the 'double slit' experiment (9). In this procedure there is a source of electrons. There is also a screen which has two slits in it. If the electrons hit the screen they get absorbed and do not go through, but if they get through one of the slits then there is another screen behind the first, and that other screen is phosphorescent, and thus shows where the electrons hit it.

One electron is sent through at a time. It is found that each electron which goes through the first screen hits at one specific place, somewhere on the further screen. There is clearly one specific place where each electron hits.

If it is worked out what is happening mathematically, what is found is very complicated and very odd. This is because different things happen, depending upon what one does. Suppose one wants to know which of the two slits the electron went through, to hit the far screen. Suppose one puts a detector near the first screen's slits, that detects which slit the electron goes through. What one finds is that the detector will indicate, for each electron, that it either went through one slit or it went through the other. This is very clear. It does not show that at any time an electron went through both slits. Each electron detected goes through either one slit or the other.

What sort of pattern builds up on the further screen if one sends many electrons through the first screen? If one looks at the pattern on the far screen, when one has the detector turned on, what one gets is two blotches, one opposite each slit, where electrons that have gone through each slit end up near each other – through one slit for one blotch, through the other slit for the other. Each is a blotch rather than a precise point of the detector screen, because in going through a slit an electron's path can deviate from a straight line. Let us assume that the slits are made close enough together so that the two blotches overlap to some extent.

Now that is when the detector is turned on. So one knows, when the detector is turned on, that each electron goes through one slit or the other. One does not get an electron going through both. It goes through one slit or the other, and there is a pattern of a blotch made by electrons going through each slit, each blotch overlapping with the other.

What happens if one then turns off the detector? Well, the overlapping double blotch disappears and one gets a pattern of lines, going across the far screen, a type of wave pattern.

If one works out the mathematics of this, it shows something very strange indeed. To derive that wave pattern of lines mathematically what one finds, with each of those electrons, is that one cannot assume it went through either one slit or the other. One cannot make that assumption.

What one *has* to assume is that it 'sort of' went through both slits. I stress the 'sort of'. The mathematics of this is associated with what assumptions one can make about the physical 'state' of each electron. The expression 'state' is used in quantum mechanics. One could say that the physical state of an electron would be its set of physical quantities, such as its speed, its mass, its position at a given time, as well as any other quantities it has.

What the correct mathematics implies is that one cannot consider each electron as having a definite physical state. One might think one would be able to say what the state of an electron is, even if one is not making any measurement. What the double slit experiment shows is that one cannot make that assumption. What it shows one must do is to assume that the only way one can talk about the 'state' of an electron is that it is a sort of 'sum of possibilities'. In this case there are two possibilities, that it goes through one slit or the other. And all one can say is that an electron's state, when one is not detecting what it is doing in the middle, is a sum of those two possibilities. One cannot say it is definitely anything. It is the 'sum' of those two things, those two possibilities (not other possibilities), but that is all it is. Importantly, when one has not detected which slit the electron is going through, one cannot say it went through either one slit or the other.

We usually assume that of course one must be able to do that, because the electron has apparently gone through that middle screen and if one puts on the detector it always shows each electron going through either one slit or the other. So it seems logical to think that with the detector off each electron will go through either one slit or the other. But no. Actually, when one is not interacting with the electron in any way, between the source and the further screen, one cannot say that it has any definite state, and that includes saying which slit it went through.

It was phenomena like this that led the physicist Richard Feynman to write that there is nobody who understands quantum mechanics. (10) There are books and books about this experiment, but it is evident that people find it almost impossible to grasp.

Now if we think of the Buddhist principle of *śunyata,* that nothing has an inherent existence, by itself, outside of relationships, the question is: is this not another very interesting parallel? Here we have a fundamental particle and what we find is that with such a particle, when we are not detecting it, we cannot say that it possesses any inherent quantities, or in Newtonian terms, any absolute quantities, at all. All we can say is that it is a sum of possibilities.

I am reminded here of one interpretation of the doctrine of *śunyata* which says that *śunyata* is not just that any phenomenon has no intrinsic existence, but also that one cannot really talk about phenomena in terms of 'existence' or 'non-existence'. What I find very interesting about the maths of quantum mechanics is that the state of an electron that one is not observing is the sum of possibilities. It is not that it does not exist, but nor can one say it exists in any particular place with any particular attributes, with any particular values. It is interesting that the maths seems to be an intriguing parallel to the Buddhist concept of *śunyata*, which of course is usually applied in a very different field.

So quantum mechanics, when we are studying fundamental particles, implies that it is problematic to think of them as having an inherent existence. This is taken further in the development of quantum mechanics called quantum field theory (QFT), which is the theory which is applied these days. In QFT the idea of a particle is further undermined, because particles are held to arise out of a 'field' (11). So one does not have electrons, one has an electron field and, regarding the number of particles the field has at any time, one cannot say that there definitely exist certain particles at any given time because QFT allows for 'virtual particles'. There are infinite possibilities of virtual particles. The whole idea of 'one particle' in QFT breaks down. And if one thinks also that perhaps the fields have intrinsic existence, really existing quantities to them, well actually they do not, because one has to apply similar 'quantum mechanical' mathematics to them, to their attributes, as one does to the attributes of particles in ordinary quantum theory. Thus the attributes of the 'field', at any given point in space and time, cannot be assumed to have a value when not measured.

To summarise, the whole idea of the intrinsic existence of particles, of fundamental particles existing inherently in themselves, has actually been breaking down. But people do not necessarily understand it like that. People can apply the mathematics, but understanding the implications is very difficult.

Quantum Mechanics and Quantum Field Theory reinforce the message about there being a lack of intrinsic existence of fundamental particles, and there is even a further quantum phenomenon called 'entanglement'. Now, in thinking about a particle, we can usually assume that it possesses a 'state' of some kind - that state might be a sum of possibilities, and that is as far as we can go – but we can usually assume that a particle has a state. But the phenomenon called entanglement shows that a particle does not necessarily have a state of its own at all. One could have millions of particles 'entangled' and only one state representing all of them, and those particles might be separated by billions of miles and if they are still entangled they are collectively represented by the same state. They are *not* separate particles although they are separated by billions of miles. Our everyday assumptions are really challenged by this, but if one reflects that there is no such thing as an intrinsically existing distance, nor intrinsically existing particle, it starts to break down one's assumptions.

Of course, somehow the quantum world gives rise to the ordinary physical world that we experience. In the ordinary world objects seem to be there in a predictable way. If my car disappeared overnight I would not think that that was due to some quantum phenomenon, I would conclude that someone had stolen it, and that it still exists somewhere. But my car is made out of those fundamental particles. So somehow, on an ordinary level, we have the everyday world with everyday properties that seem to persist when we do not perceive them, but it is a manifestation of a quantum physical world where the same statements are not true. This apparent discrepancy is fascinating.

However, my main point is that quantum mechanics and relativity have very interesting parallels with the doctrine of *śunyata* – that no phenomenon has an intrinsic existence of its own. Everything exists within relationships. One cannot talk about any phenomenon, such as a fundamental particle, or any attribute such as distance or time, as actually having an intrinsic existence.

Now, returning to the idea of physical laws, to me it seems that an underlying assumption to the concept of 'physical laws' is that they 'determine' what happens. It also appears to me that modern science is getting quite a long way away from the idea of deterministic physical laws. It seems to be getting to a more 'open' idea of conditionality – that there are patterns of phenomena, inter-relationships of phenomena, very complicated patterns that depend at times on the observations of people observing those patterns, but that reality just cannot be so deterministic. Yes, there is conditionality, and there are patterns of conditionality, understandable in complex mathematical ways – but actually everything is to some extent just 'open'. Moreover, the mathematics of quantum mechanics is actually expressed in terms of probabilities. I think the implication of all this is that there is much more to the universe than one might think or expect, and that one should also not think in terms of there being 'universal laws' of physics, particularly deterministic ones.

I am going to finish this chapter with a couple of quotations, bringing in a further parallel between modern physics and Buddhism. The first is from Martin Rees, the Astronomer Royal:

"An astonishing concept has entered mainstream cosmological thought: physical reality could be hugely more extensive than the patch of space and time traditionally called "the universe." We've learnt that we live in a solar system that is just one planetary system among billions, in one galaxy among billions. But there are signs that a further Copernican demotion confronts us. The entire panorama that astronomers can observe could be a tiny part of the aftermath of our Big Bang, which is itself just one bang among a potentially infinite ensemble. In this grander perspective, what we've traditionally called the laws of nature may be no more than parochial bylaws—local manifestations of "bedrock" laws that must be sought at a still deeper level." (12)

The second is from the Avatamsaka Sutra, a large Mahayana Buddhist Sutra that became very influential in Far Eastern Buddhism. This is an excerpt from many pages of similar material. It is a description of parts of the universe. It uses the terminology of a 'Buddha Field', which is a system of worlds in which a Buddha has appeared:

"...Turning to the right of this Sphere of Inexhaustible Light sea of fragrant water, there is a sea of fragrant water called Diamond Flame Light, with a system of worlds called Repository of Arrays of Buddha Halos, composed of voices extolling the names of all Buddhas. At the bottom of this world system is a world called Jewel Flame Lotus, shaped like a curl of hair, the colour of crystal, resting on a sea of whirlpools of the colours of all jewels, covered by clouds of palaces of all adornments, surrounded by as many worlds as atoms in a Buddha-field.

Above this, past as many worlds as atoms in a Buddha-field, is a world called Repository of flames of Light; the Buddha there is called Light of Unhindered Independent Wisdom.

Above this, past as many worlds as atoms in a Buddha-field, is a world called Beautiful Array of Jewelled Discs; the Buddha there is called Light of All Jewels.

Above this...." (13)

The Avatamsaka Sutra is rather poetic and mythological in its description, but the point to understand is that, in contrast to the early western tradition – of the Earth surrounded by planetary spheres and then god's heaven – since the start of Buddhism its conception of the universe has been utterly vast. Moreover, in the Avatamsaka Sutra there is the implicit suggestion that there are completely different realms of nature, not just this particular physical world and its particular physical laws, or rather particular patterns of conditionality. The Avatamsaka Sutra is also talking in terms of there being Buddhas in other world systems, the implication being that Enlightenment can arise within sentient beings wherever in the universe the conditions are favourable.

8

Summary and Further Thoughts

The systems of ideas that people internalise have major effects upon their ability, or inability, to understand the world and act appropriately and ethically within it. Systems of ideas are rather like the human brain's versions of computer software. They enable us to think and act, and can be useful, appropriate and positive in their effects upon human understanding and behaviour. They can also be useless, inappropriate and harmful, somewhat like the viruses that subvert computer functioning.

With regard to the systems of ideas in Western thought, it is very important to emphasise that there have been major positive developments. One could summarise the two key positive developments as being, firstly, the rise of empirical science and, secondly, what I have come to call, after Cicero, the theory and practice of 'humanitas', by which I mean the recognition of the existence of a natural morality, especially including humaneness, tolerance, and consideration of others.

Each of these key developments was a healthy movement away from the ancient Christian monotheistic tradition of revelation, and each came about at least in part because of the rediscovery and revival of classical pagan thought. Each was associated with the idea of there being natural laws, whether scientific or moral.

It is vital to acknowledge and celebrate the positives in Western thought. The development of empirical science has given the human race many benefits, including increased abilities to overcome poverty, malnourishment and disease. The theory and practice of humanitas, including the ideas and practices that developed in association with it (ideas of human rights, democracy, liberty, the individual, and tolerance), have had major beneficial consequences as they have been increasingly put into effect. It should also be acknowledged, and celebrated, that there was a vital aspect of the Christian tradition which linked into, and became a driving force within, the developing theory and practice of humanitas. This was the teaching of Jesus. It was exemplified in the abolition of slavery.

However, sadly, there have been negative aspects to the development of western thought. The main set of these is closely associated with physicalism, by which I mean the belief that human behaviour and human systems can be explained by natural laws very like those of Newtonian physics. Much of this way of thinking developed in the nineteenth century and persisted throughout the twentieth.

When I first began to seriously investigate the history of Western thought I did not realise the extent and importance of physicalism, nor how so many negative effects stemmed from it. Indeed, discovering the dominance of physicalism has been a surprise. This dominance is reflected in striking similarities, across disciplines and subject areas, in the physicalist ideas employed. It is also reflected in the persistent influence, into this century, of systems of ideas, such as neoclassical economics, which stem from physicalist assumptions.

Associated with physicalism, although also somewhat distinct from it, is another form of scientism, social evolutionism, which has also had serious adverse effects. This developed in the context of the rise of physicalism. However, it contained ideas and beliefs which derived partly from theories about species evolution, partly from political ideas about struggle between nations and ethnic groups, and also partly from old beliefs about there being set stages through which the human world evolves, beliefs that go back at least as far as Augustine. (Theories about species evolution were also themselves influenced by physicalism and political beliefs about struggle and progress.)

Between them, physicalism and social evolutionism have had major negative consequences in political thought - across the political spectrum. They have between them underpinned Marxism, ethnic nationalism, Nazism, and neoclassical economics. The last of these has led to financial crises, and to very damaging predatory and parasitic financial and economic practices. The others have contributed strongly to the arising of two world wars, and to the barbaric and genocidal treatment of those believed to be in the wrong group, whether the wrong ethnic or social group. Physicalism also adversely affected the development of disciplines such as psychology, psychotherapy, sociology and management theory, and it has had major negative consequences in the field of economics, where its underlying assumptions still appear to be dominant.

Closely associated with the development of physicalism was the growth of materialist atheism. Given the increasing influence of the physical sciences, including biology, it is unsurprising that the reaction away from theism, especially revelatory theism, was very strongly influenced by the rise of physical science, so that a materialist philosophy became an integral part of western atheism. However, materialism is in itself a belief system, one which rests on unproven assumptions. Materialist arguments are also typically expressed in ways which render them apparently unfalsifiable, thereby contradicting a commonly held understanding about scientific method. So attempted materialist explanations of consciousness are always very vague about how the brain supposedly produces consciousness, a vagueness masked by the confused use of inappropriate philosophical or neuro-scientific language. Accompanying this, evidence against the materialist belief system is usually dismissed through a combination of ad hominem arguments, argument by abuse, and faulty logic.

The development of physicalism in a theistic context, and the associated rise of materialist atheism, led in general to the restricted choice of 'god or nothing but physical matter'. This restricted choice limited thinking about religious and spiritual issues, and also strongly affected moral philosophy as well as the philosophy of mind. Religion came to be seen as either involving belief in god, or else belief in no spiritual reality; morality came to be seen as either involving god's moral laws, or else moral relativism; the range of possible ideas about the nature of consciousness came to be seen as either belief in a soul or else belief that consciousness is just an aspect of physical matter.

Physicalism is related to the idea that there exist natural laws. Theories of natural law were characteristically rather 'determinist'. This partly reflects the nature of Newtonian physics (in contrast to quantum mechanics), but also partly reflects theistic conceptions of a god as universal creator and ruler who makes everything happen, and who even preordains everything (as in the doctrine of 'predestination'). Such determinism was expressed particularly in social evolutionism, where specific stages of progress or evolution of society were assumed to inevitably occur. Precisely which stages were believed to happen was associated with the political outlook of the person proposing the theory.

Such determinism was also associated with something which in the pre-computer age people could not do. This was to analyse 'non-linear' processes. The mathematical equations of non-linear processes are usually effectively impossible to solve without having computers to perform the often huge number of computations required. Moreover, the precise behaviour of non-linear processes is often very difficult to predict in advance, even with computers. In effect, before the computer age people were constrained to think in terms of 'linear' processes, which are much more predictable. The overall result, when considering human systems, was to think in simplistic terms, assuming that how those systems behave could be reasonably well predicted. Accompanying this was an emphasis upon measurement. However, much vitally important qualitative knowledge can be lost if one endeavours to reduce our ways of understanding to what, supposedly, can be 'measured'.

With regard to the negative developments in Western thought, it is worthwhile to ask what influences they have in the contemporary world. How much do these key negative ideas influence us now? In pondering this question I have to come to recognise that they are still influential within various academic disciplines, and through them the world at large. Importantly, they manifest within political thought, throughout the political spectrum. Together they seriously limit contemporary thinking to a restricted set of choices, and have been undermining the positive traditions of Western thought.

Thus, if we consider economics and business, it is sobering to realise that neoclassical economics is still dominant, although coming under increasing criticism. It did, in its most typical form, fall out of favour after the great depression of the thirties, with Keynesian economics becoming influential after the Second World War, but problems with that, and serious inflation, led to its resurgence in the nineteen eighties. Businesses and government also still appear to be strongly affected by the tradition of management practice stemming ultimately from 'scientific management'. As I mentioned in chapter five, this tradition has certain characteristics, including: a preoccupation with measurement (including 'targets') rather than good qualitative knowledge; poor understanding of the actual needs and practices of the specific business or organisation being managed; and 'top-down' control ignoring the expertise, knowledge and opinions of those lower down in the hierarchy (1).

Both neoclassical economics and problematic management theory promote serious misunderstandings about how economies and businesses function well. The irony here is that such approaches, which supposedly developed to promote good understanding and practice of economics and business, have actually had opposite, damaging, effects. Thus higher management, as well as government and civil service practice, too often became ignorant meddling from above, deficient in 'domain knowledge', preoccupied with inappropriate measurement, and obsessed with the 'bottom line'. This has resulted in the failure of many successful companies, and in the undermining of national systems such as health care and education (2). Associated with this approach there has been the growth of excessive and inappropriate regulation and inspection. As someone who has worked over the course of decades in the National Health Service, I recognise this pattern in the way successive governments have imposed upon the NHS increasingly harmful control from above, undermining clinical staff and making working within it increasingly difficult and stressful. A recent set of interviews with some NHS chief executives illustrates these issues (3).

Neoclassical economics and management theory tend to be identified as having associations with 'right wing' political views, at least when the term 'right wing' is used with one of its various contradictory meanings, referring to belief in, and promotion of, the unregulated 'free market' and associated business practice. Meanwhile, in another part of the political spectrum, usually considered 'left wing', in the last half of the twentieth century there were major influences of other systems of damaging ideas which stem from the negative developments I have discussed. In this regard, it is worthwhile to consider how social evolutionism and Marxism have each influenced Western thought since the Second World War.

Social evolutionism has had a major but indirect effect. Western thought and political practice over the last sixty years or so have been strongly affected by what one could call the 'flight from social evolutionism', which includes the flight from ethnic nationalism and Nazism. For decades these political belief systems became thoroughly discredited, and on the whole were not taken seriously. Generally, political parties associated with them (usually referred to as 'far right') became very unpopular. Associated with this, the legitimacy of the concept of the nation state was undermined. (More recently, however, there has been the re-emergence of nationalist and 'far right' parties.)

Alongside this political development, specific ideas associated with social evolutionism were also either discredited or very strongly criticised. These included the old belief in 'survival of the fittest', the theory and practice of eugenics, and also any hypothesised strong influence of genetics upon human behaviour. This has contributed to a strident emphasis within the social sciences upon the belief that social and cultural conditioning (and not genetics) have the strongest influences upon human behaviour. There has been, in effect, a dominant assumption that a human being is, for the most part, a 'blank slate' upon which social and cultural conditioning, including that stemming from the economic and industrial system, have the major effects. One consequence of this assumption is the common belief that, if a group of people are in some way worse off than others, this must be due to the 'system' i.e. to cultural and economic factors within the Western world. (Such an approach also ignores or downplays the consequences brought about by an individual's or a group's own actions.)

In addition to this strong, indirect influence of social evolutionism, through the flight away from it, there has been a continued more direct influence of Marxism. Whilst much of Western Europe had experienced the effects of Nazi occupation, it had not experienced Soviet occupation. This difference allowed Marxism to have a continued legitimacy amongst many people in the West, despite the appalling genocidal behaviour of Marxist governments. Given the economic depression of the thirties, which left many people very disillusioned with the Western economic system, the Marxist alternative was given further apparent legitimacy. In particular, there was the growth of the 'New Left', who advanced ideas based upon Marxism within academia and the world at large, ideas that were taken very seriously.

One aspect of this was postmodernism. This was primarily a movement in ideas involving a denial of the concept of objective truth. It developed and became a dominant force in many university departments in the latter half of the twentieth century. Postmodernism has its origins in Marxism, and particularly in the Marxist dismissal of morality and truth as rationalisations of bourgeois beliefs and behaviour. It has contributed strongly to the belief that each cultural group has its own, equally valid, views of the world (and associated practices) which are not criticisable from a Western standpoint nor from any overall objective position.

Moreover, Marxism itself has had, from its beginnings, the aim to overthrow the 'bourgeoisie', who are seen as a class of oppressors, and who are generally demonised. (This Marxist anti-bourgeois prejudice was closely paralleled by the antisemitism within Nazism.)

This has subsequently led to an implicit, stereotyped agenda that often occurs when issues of disadvantage are taken up. This is that there must be an oppressive group who are deemed to be deliberately exploiting or harming the disadvantaged – an oppressive group who should be actively overcome. This implicit agenda has been very influential. It is also often associated with the belief that disadvantage is caused by the Western cultural and economic 'system'.

Associated with the flight from social evolutionism, and with the continued influence of Marxism, there is also what I have come to refer to as 'Western guilt', by which I mean a feeling of irrational guilt about Western culture. This is in part guilt about social evolutionism and its consequences, including two world wars, Nazism and the holocaust, and its use in legitimising colonialism. It is also in part guilt about the negative effects of the Western economic system. Such guilt added a strong emotional impetus to the flight from social evolutionism and to the belief that the Western economic system was inherently bad. This strengthened the appeal of Marxism, especially for many middle class Western intellectuals. In particular, the belief developed that 'Western imperialism' is the primary evil in the world. This is in effect what one could call an 'anti-Westernism'.

This anti-Westernism, combined with the belief that other cultures cannot be criticised from a Western, or objective, standpoint, has contributed to what can be termed 'the cultural double standard'. This is typified by a focus upon faults in Western culture whilst ignoring its positives, alongside a reverse focus upon the positives in non-Western cultures, and avoidance of considering their negatives.

One phenomenon which has been affected by this cultural double standard is the movement to combat what came to be known as 'racism'.

In many ways combatting racism has been a very positive development. This has involved working against ethnic hatred, and associated ethnic prejudice and discrimination. Given that these had been powerful factors in Western culture during the nineteenth and early twentieth centuries, such a development was necessary and welcome. However, the term 'racism' came to be predominantly associated with Western, and especially white people's, prejudice against other ethnic groups. It tended to ignore other forms of ethnic hatred, prejudice and discrimination. This particular aspect of the cultural double standard has become so pronounced that one could even put it that the term 'racist' is itself racist. In other words, it promotes a biased focus upon whites' prejudice against non-whites, whilst ignoring the many instances of ethnic hatred, prejudice and discrimination perpetrated by non-white people. This is also an example of what, in chapter one, I termed the political dynamic of 'inverted prejudice'.

Furthermore, such inverted prejudice, associated with the implicit agenda coming from Marxism, has also become common at other times when there are issues of inequality and social injustice. Given that societies can contain groups who are disadvantaged, discriminated against, or exploited, for example the 'untouchables' in Hinduism, inequality and social injustice, and their opposites, are very important issues. Working in a principled way to overcome a group's disadvantage or mistreatment is both appropriate and commendable.

Unfortunately, too often this is not what happens. Instead the stereotypical pattern of 'oppressed and oppressors' (coming from Marxism) is applied to groups who are actually or supposedly disadvantaged, as well as to the groups who are in some way their opposites. Associated with this dynamic, the call for 'equality' often comes to mean something quite different - the inversion of inequality. In other words, working for 'equality' can mean instead striving to make the 'oppressed' group advantaged, with the 'oppressing' group being discriminated against (and thereby made to suffer social injustice). This is often referred to as the encouragement of 'tolerance' (towards the disadvantaged groups), but it involves intolerance towards the supposed oppressors. Associated with this there is typically much hatred, a characteristic which reflects that of the Marxism from which comes the stereotype of 'oppression'.

In particular, this hateful stereotypical pattern often manifests as an implicit, and at times quite explicit, selection of prejudices against the supposed oppressors, who may be westerners, the middle class, men, or heterosexuals, as well as groups who embody a combination of one or more of these attributes (4).

Inverted inequality, and the promotion of one-sided 'tolerance', are now being actively promoted within European nations by the 'European Framework National Statute for the Promotion of Tolerance'. This includes the following:

"The special protection afforded to members of vulnerable and disadvantaged groups may imply a preferential treatment. Strictly speaking, this preferential treatment goes beyond mere respect and acceptance lying at the root of tolerance." (5)

This document also prescribes a compulsory 'rehabilitation programme' for those who put forward a viewpoint deemed offensive. 'Anti-feminism' is one such viewpoint, and thus criticising feminism becomes a crime. The promotion of 'tolerance', but only towards supposed 'vulnerable and disadvantaged groups', is also to be promoted within the education system, in adult education and professional training, and in the media.

This political dynamic also often involves false analysis of inequality and social injustice, both by ignoring real examples and inventing others. For example, it has typically ignored social injustice in non-Western cultures (although this is beginning to change to some extent). The almost complete lack of consideration in the West of the appalling treatment of untouchables is a glaring example. Indeed, to criticise such injustice could itself be seen as 'racist', as it is criticising a non-Western culture. Alongside this there can be an untruthful and highly biased consideration of evidence of supposed discrimination or maltreatment in Western cultures. (For example, there is often an exclusive focus upon domestic violence against women, perpetrated by Western men, so that domestic violence tends to be believed to be something men do to women. This approach ignores completely the comparable level of domestic violence perpetrated against men by Western women.)

These days such political activity also makes a virtue out of taking offence. Criticism of real or supposed disadvantaged groups, or their cultures, is forbidden, and is deemed 'offensive' or considered to be 'hate speech'. This is a modern equivalent of blasphemy. It is often described as the 'promotion of tolerance' when in fact it is the opposite. Members of the supposed oppressive group are also labelled as being 'privileged', which is then used as a rationalisation for denying them any expression of opinion (or any rights). However, any hateful criticism of supposed oppressive groups (provided they are Western) is allowed and encouraged. Thus, as I have already described, the 'tolerance' promoted can be very one sided, with the supposedly disadvantaged groups and their cultures being 'tolerated', and any criticism of them, or expression of a different view, being suppressed. This political activity actually parallels, or embodies, a Marxist practice put forward by Herbert Marcuse in his essay 'Repressive Tolerance' (6). In this he wrote: "…the realization of the objective of tolerance would call for intolerance toward prevailing policies, attitudes, opinions…" Such activity also seriously undermines the very important human right of freedom of speech.

One important consequence of the cultural double standard, in association with the political dynamic of inverted prejudice, is that it has become very difficult to argue an intellectual defence of the positives in Western culture generally, and in specific Western nations. Associated with this there has also been a difficulty defending the concept of the nation state, at least if the nation is Western. Nationalism has come to be usually identified as 'far right' politically. In Europe this has been an important aspect of the development of the European Union. However, the EU has now developed to a point where its leadership can override democratically elected national governments – yet that leadership is not itself democratically answerable to the electorates of Europe. This serious democratic deficit, combined with high levels of immigration, is now provoking a strong backlash, as a large proportion of Europe's population feel seriously threatened, especially when militant Islamic fundamentalism has been increasing. In Western Europe this feeling of being threatened has not been helped by the cultural double standard and associated inverted prejudice having effectively silenced debate. Moreover, in Eastern Europe, memories of being subject to the Soviet Union have been re-awakened in people now finding themselves ruled undemocratically by the EU. In consequence, many people are turning to nationalist or 'far right' political parties.

One could sum up the current state of politics in the Western world as one of profound crisis. Voters increasingly distrust the old politics, as well as the political class that rules them, and are searching for an alternative. Yet political thinking is locked into the stereotypes of the past. Thus, in general the harmful ideas of the nineteenth century continue to have strong influences upon our political, social and economic thinking. Social evolutionism has, in particular, an indirect influence through the reaction away from it, especially as this manifested in the flight from ethnic nationalism. This undermined consideration of the positives in the nation state, in Western nations and Western culture. Marxism and physicalism continue to have more direct influences. The offshoots of Marxism have undermined genuine concern for, and practice of, tolerance and social justice, as well as promulgated an anti-Western prejudice. Physicalism, through neoclassical economics and management theory, continues to undermine economic and business functioning. (Its influence on Marxism should also not be forgotten.)

One major implication of all this is that political ideas, throughout the political spectrum, that stem from physicalism and other harmful nineteenth and twentieth century ideologies, should be seen through and transcended. This development needs to involve moving away from simplistic and highly misleading concepts such as 'left' and 'right', 'socialist' and 'capitalist', which have arisen from physicalist and associated dogmas. We need a new approach to understanding social, economic and political issues that is free of the old nonsense, that protects and emphasises the positives in the western tradition, and which is not an elaborate rationalisation of resentment. It would also be very helpful to develop this approach by building upon the positive developments in Western tradition using both good contemporary non-physicalist knowledge and Buddhist understanding and practice.

The real practice of humanitas, with its genuine application in human rights and the other practices that I mentioned, is of central importance here. This crucial development in Western thought needs to be re-emphasised. It is still there within Western nations, to some extent, although it is increasingly under threat. A healthy society needs to be based upon the practice of humanitas. Such practice is in effect that of natural ethics. Thus a new approach needs to explicitly base itself upon natural ethics and the recognition that societies are healthy to the extent that the people within them are ethically, and psychologically, healthy. Its aims need to be the encouragement, nurturing and protection of ethical and psychological health. Within that context it needs to recognise the importance of appropriate levels of economic well-being. This is really the continuation and extension of the positives in the Western tradition.

A very important aspect of such an approach is the recognition, encouragement and nurturing of positive relationships of all kinds. This includes relationships within the family, at work, and between people and public servants and politicians. A healthy society involves networks of good relationships between people. By a 'good' relationship I mean one which is ethical and nurtures psychological (and physical) health and well-being. Two areas of knowledge are particularly important here – the Buddhist understanding of the ethical dimension to psychology, as well as contemporary understanding within psychology and therapy of the importance of healthy attachments and psychological health in general.

A network of such relationships is very different from what could be called a society of 'top-down isolation', in which people's links with others are negative, poor or non-existent, and in which there is what could be termed a 'culture of imposition from above', where rules of behaviour are imposed from the top and enforced through bullying and punishment down a hierarchy of power, through tenuous and inadequate relationships. A healthy society is also different from a culture in which people do have close ties with each other but in which each person has to 'fit-in' to rigid norms of behaviour and belief or else be punished in some way.

I have explicitly used the term 'network' here, as that is, in one way or another, what sets of relationships together constitute. I am also aware, when using the term, of the study of networks in complexity theory. In understanding and analysing such networks one needs to consider the qualities of the relationships – especially how ethical and psychologically healthy they are. Such analysis will give a very clear and necessary understanding of vital aspects of a given society or of the groups within it. This is also an analysis very different to those stemming from nineteenth century physicalism and the political ideas associated with that. It does not just analyse society into individuals and groups (with strong emphasis upon either the individual or the group, depending upon the political persuasion of the person doing the analysis). Instead it highlights the relationships which individuals have, and also presents a picture of how any group of people is actually constituted, and how healthily it functions. This is very different from just bringing to mind a set of people, as a whole or as individuals. It immediately brings to the fore issues which otherwise would tend to be forgotten. (Thinking in such a way can be helped, for example, by taking any specific group and imaginatively or symbolically representing each person in it by a circle, and each relationship by a line between two circles, with the nature and quality of that relationship represented by, say, colours. Immediately one does this, one is considering very important aspects of individual and group functioning.)

It is also important to consider similar network analysis as a vital part of understanding the functioning of, and relationships between, groups and organisations of all kinds, including nations. In general, what one could call 'qualitative network analysis' can focus upon key aspects of human behaviour, both individual and collective.

A new approach to social and political understanding also needs to be able to acknowledge those aspects of any particular old political doctrine that are reasonably correct and positive, and to distinguish them from the false and harmful. This involves analysing the various political approaches such as socialism, liberalism and conservatism, and asking what is positive and negative within each of these traditions. Proceeding in such a way transcends harmful stereotypical (and emotive) thinking, for example in terms of 'right' and 'left', where someone immediately jumps to a clichéd opinion of another person's position, and dismisses it out of hand, typically by applying a label to that person with whom they disagree. This also requires honesty, and not the motivated misrepresentation of evidence. Overall it is an approach which escapes the restricted choices and stereotypical thinking of the politics that has developed from the nineteenth century onwards.

Such an approach also involves acknowledging what is positive and appropriate in specific concepts and practices, such as the 'nation state', 'human rights', 'individual liberty', 'freedom of speech' and 'equality', amongst others, whilst recognising what may be harmful or false in the concepts themselves, or in their practice. For example, with regard to the nation state, its positives need to be recognised, such as the importance of a shared 'home' in which people can safely and tolerantly live together, and over which they have collective responsibility and control. On the other hand, the harm arising from ethnic nationalism and ethnic hatred needs to be acknowledged. Or consider freedom of speech. This is a vital human right, which protects the practice of honesty and the freedom to believe what one considers true. This includes the right for people to say what they will, even if one thoroughly disagrees with that. The only exception to freedom of speech should be the deliberate incitement to violence against other people. What is not healthy, and actually seriously threatens freedom of speech, is the practice of taking offence, which is being increasingly used as a rationalisation to criminalise opinions. In any case, taking offence is itself an immoral action, which often indicates serious resentment.

A new approach also needs to be able to distinguish between good business and economic practice, and harmful. Hopefully a wider understanding of the implications of complexity theory will in itself undermine commonly held false assumptions of physicalism, and help pave the way for a much better understanding of human systems, including economic systems. In particular, it would be good if 'free market' ideas were replaced by what one could call a 'complex market' approach to understanding economic systems. This could be associated with appropriate, non-physicalist psychological understanding of how human beings really do behave.

This issue is particularly important because of globalisation and its effects. Multinational companies are often now in effect 'transnational', existing beyond the influence of national and international laws. They are also able, in their own interest, to subvert or strongly influence those laws, and the governments that enact them. Such activity needs appropriate understanding and analysis, as well as the development of appropriate means of international regulation and control.

Going beyond physicalism could also help overcome foolish ideas and methods in management theory and practice. Such poor management is paralleled by poor governance - activity by government ministers and civil servants that has the same faults. Ministers can enact and impose policies in ways which display little domain knowledge, and which ignore the opinions of those with such knowledge, especially those who will have to implement the policies. Such poor practice typically includes inappropriate and invalid forms of measurement, especially the targets so beloved of politicians, senior managers and civil servants.

Overcoming such poor management (and government) practice will also involve movement away from what is often an accompanying culture of bullying, towards a management culture with a moral basis, where relationships between managers and those under them are recognised as very important, and where compassion and mindfulness are recognised as vital aspects of good practice. Alongside this, what one could call the 'entrepreneurial spirit' needs to be acknowledged and encouraged, but distinguished clearly from both poor management and harmful, greed-based business practice. Also, the importance of 'domain knowledge' in management and government practice needs to be re-emphasised.

With regard to government, questions about relationships are also central when one considers issues of people's representation and participation in government. Political parties have in the West tended to become divorced from the electorate, with the emergence of a political class keen to protect its own interests. Thus the relationships between electors and elected have become tenuous. With the rise of quangos, partly answerable to government but not directly to the electorate, ordinary people's influence over the institutions governing them has significantly decreased. (This has been particularly the case in the European Union.) An important question is how the electorate can regain its influence upon a political and bureaucratic elite.

Related to this issue, there are other important ones for democracy. These are questions of regulation and control. Such practices are often vital, in order to minimise harm, whether this be intentional or accidental. However, it appears that the types of regulation and control adopted can be detrimental. For example, in a health care system an emphasis upon targets in respect of 'waiting lists' can lead to neglect elsewhere in the system, as resources are diverted to lower waiting list times. When inappropriate targets are set from on-high by politicians with little domain knowledge, and distant quangos investigate whether they are being met by sending in squads of inspectors with no relationships to the people working, this results in those people, such as teachers and health service staff, having little say or little control over their own work, and significantly increased pressure upon them. It is in effect a system of bullying. Such methods of regulation often lead to poorer practice, not better, as targets are met to the detriment of aspects of actual good practice.

So politicians and senior civil servants impose their decisions on senior managers, who in turn have to impose inappropriate decisions and control over their staff. The politicians who control and regulate from above are then criticised by journalists and the populace at large when standards fall or targets are not met. Thus there exists a feedback loop, made up of tenuous but negative relationships. One could call it a cycle of bullying.

On the other hand, lack of external regulation and inspection can also lead to poor practice, or allow it to happen. Self-serving businesses, organisations and workforces can develop, to the harm of others, when not scrutinised adequately. However, such an issue also applies to the organisations, and the people working in them, whose job is regulation and inspection. Who inspects and regulates them? There is no guaranteed solution to this problem, especially when relationship networks between organisations are tenuous and poor.

The answer can never be just a matter of having particular institutions and practices in place, to scrutinise, regulate and control. Whilst such activities are at times very important, there is always the question of the morality of the people who work in those institutions and apply those practices. This implies the necessity of widespread recognition of the importance of natural ethics. Alongside this, there is the importance of the development and protection of networks of positive relationships, between organisations, and between the people working within them.

Overall, there is the very serious question of the appropriateness of any system of regulation, inspection and control. It is very easy to pursue such activities incorrectly – by doing them too much, too little, or in very inappropriate ways.

Related to these issues are those of policing and defence. Unfortunately, pacifism and abdication from using violence do not necessarily, or even often, lead to the overcoming of violence and criminality generally. Instead they leave power in the hands of those who are prepared to cause harm to get what they want. Whilst having a human world that contains little violence is a very important and worthwhile goal, moving towards that goal is neither simple nor straightforward. Pragmatically, the important questions are how can violence and harm be reduced, and how can people be reasonably protected from them. Having a police force, as well as armed forces for defence, to fulfil these roles, then raises the question of how these carry out their work appropriately and well, and how they too should be scrutinised. What are the 'checks and balances' that need to be in place to ensure good practice? It is important that these are appropriate.

Complexity theory, however, shows that there are often no easy solutions, and that well-intentioned actions can have results which are the opposite of those intended. Moreover, the human world is forever changing, amongst other things through scientific and technological developments and their consequences. Today's solution may be tomorrow's problem. The 'checks and balances' that may keep today's society functioning well (assuming that they do) may tomorrow be inadequate to the task. In a dynamic, ever-changing culture, dynamic, ever-changing checks and balances are needed. Furthermore, complexity theory shows that rigid control of a system, and complete absence of control, can both be harmful.

Nevertheless, although complexity theory shows that there often are no easy solutions, it is far better to try to understand complex systems appropriately than by using physicalist-based theories that completely misunderstand how such systems function, and whose applications thereby make things worse.

Moving on from political issues, what then of possible developments in philosophical, religious and scientific thought? What developments could there be, and how could Buddhism contribute to these?

Viewed from a Buddhist perspective, the positive ideas of the Western natural moral law tradition have been steps towards the appreciation and practice of the natural ethics at the heart of genuine Buddhism. Furthermore, the exposition of ideas of natural law more generally can be seen as steps towards awareness of the Buddhist principle of conditionality. Overall, natural law thinking can be understood as an implicit movement towards awareness of the underlying moral, spiritual and metaphysical principles that Buddhism recognises, although these principles have been interpreted within a non-Buddhist framework that has been strongly influenced by theism and by the rise of physical science. This affinity between Buddhism and positive aspects of Western thought implies that new positive developments can come out of the meeting and intermingling of the two traditions. Moreover, as I discussed briefly at the ends of chapters five and six, I consider that nowadays we might be on the cusp of a major change in how the universe is understood, involving the overturning of physicalism and materialism, and associated with developments in modern science and the influence of Buddhism. This leads to the question as to what would be the important points of meeting and cross-fertilisation between the positive Western tradition and Buddhism?

Firstly, the natural law tradition is still there to some extent within science, with the idea of 'laws of nature' on occasion also explicitly used, even by materialist atheists. The Buddhist understanding of conditionality provides a deep rationale for science, one that overlaps with, but goes beyond, natural law thinking.

Secondly, modern physical science has also overturned earlier scientific ideas, ones that became associated with physicalism. Moving beyond physicalism is an important issue for modern thought in general, in order to overcome its harmful legacies, and so that similar negative consequences are less likely to happen in future. Associated with this is the need to move beyond the restricted choice of 'god or nothing but physical matter'. Buddhism is intrinsically non-physicalist, non-materialist, and non-theistic.

Thirdly, away from a religious context the concept of the existence of natural moral law has faded, except implicitly within the idea of human rights. The Buddhist understanding of conditionality and natural ethics can both support human rights and revitalise moral thinking.

Then there are other specific issues. Buddhist understandings of meditation, consciousness and ethics could dovetail into modern non-physicalist and complexity-based thinking, complementing and extending it. This is already evident to some extent in psychology, with the spread of Buddhist mindfulness practice. However, the study of the natural ethical aspects of individual, group and system functioning would be an important aspect of a non-physicalist approach, in psychology and in other disciplines. As I have already discussed, such an approach can inform thinking about politics and political theories.

An important issue, however, is to avoid the reinterpretation of Buddhist ideas and practices in terms of the 'restricted choice'. Thus the 'secular mindfulness' movement, i.e. the application of mindfulness divorced from its Buddhist context, is in part developing into a 'secular Buddhism' movement, reinterpreting the Buddha's teachings as if they were the same as modern materialist atheism. Such a development is basically a 'dumbing down' of Buddhism, and a profound misunderstanding and misrepresentation of what it is.

However, in contrast to ideas stemming from physicalism and the restricted choice, there could develop forms of scientific and related study based upon a radical acceptance of the non-material existence of consciousness. By 'radical acceptance' I mean accepting that the nature and existence of consciousness cannot be explained in terms of physical matter. Such post-materialist science could perhaps include the development of a suitable non-materialist conceptualisation of consciousness. This would be associated with appropriate forms of exploration and study with regard to the nature and structure of consciousness. Deep meditation is likely to be a crucial element in such exploration and study.

Modern physics, with its apparent implicit critique of ideas of inherent substance, could also perhaps be influenced by Buddhist principles in its future developments. I discussed the interesting parallels between the doctrine of emptiness and modern physical theory. Perhaps, if these parallels are more than just parallels, and are indicators that the Buddhist doctrine of emptiness is reflected in the theories of relativity and quantum mechanics, then the doctrine of emptiness might help provide ideas in the further development of such 'deep theory' in physics. By 'deep theory' I mean the theory of underlying patterns of conditionality, usually referred to as 'laws of physics', such as quantum mechanics and relativity and the various theories of particle physics. Perhaps this could be associated with mathematics which is not based upon assuming the independent existence of discrete things, but upon considering relationships as primary. (Topos theory is a development within mathematics which does this.). Whether or not that is the case, it seems important that any new physics recognises that it is problematic to assume the independent existence of entities which are not in relationship with other aspects of the physical world, but instead emphasises the primary importance of the relationships.

A radical appreciation of openness, emptiness and conditionality could also lead to deeper understanding in many areas of thought, not just in the physical sciences but in the study of human behaviour and human systems. This could complement complexity theory. Such an approach would be very different to that based upon physicalism, materialism, and ideas of natural law with underlying determinist assumptions. In contrast, such a new approach would be pragmatic, with an acceptance of indeterminacy and unpredictability, and with an awareness of the conditional nature of specific patterns of relationship between phenomena. Perhaps one could term such an approach 'conditionalist'. In my seventh chapter I quoted Martin Rees, who wrote of a new 'Copernican revolution' with regard to ideas about the extent and nature of the physical universe. Actually a more thorough-going revolution in thinking is likely to be based upon the radical acceptance of consciousness, combined with post-physicalist, conditionalist thinking. Maybe one could also characterise this as an approach involving 'pragmatic empiricism' and 'natural morality'.

The philosopher John Rawls, in his book 'The Theory of Justice' described a thought experiment containing something called 'the original position'. This is a hypothetical position in which people are asked to decide what society should be like, when they are placed in a 'veil of ignorance' where: *"No one knows his place in society, his class position or social status, nor does anyone know his fortune in the distribution of natural assets and abilities, his intelligence, strength, and the like."* (7) In other words, people are asked to imagine they are going to be born in a society, without knowing in advance where they will be born within it, and are then asked what institutions and laws there should be in that society. Rawls used that thought experiment to argue that people so placed would choose to live in a society of fairness and equality. (Whether or not they would is itself an interesting question.)

Rawls' 'original position', with its 'veil of ignorance', is hypothetical. But suppose that it were real. After all, there are in fact many instances around the world of children remembering past lives (8). If the Buddhist doctrine of re-becoming (or 'rebirth') is true then actually we will be reborn without knowing in advance where and in what circumstances. If that is the case, then into what type of society do we wish to be reborn?

Rebirth is the traditional Buddhist theory about what one could call the 'continuity of consciousness'. It is a theory which involves postulating that the processes of consciousness that make us up, along with the physical processes of our body, continue in some way after bodily death. The physical processes that make up our body change at death, but do not just disappear into nothingness. Moreover, if we have had children then our DNA continues, at least in part. There is no logical reason why the processes of consciousness should disappear into nothingness either. Although they are strongly influenced by the physical nervous system during life, they are not physical processes, nor made up of physical matter. To assume they are somehow created out of nothing during pregnancy, and then disappear into nothing at death, is actually quite odd, rather like assuming that the physical body comes out of nothing and disappears into nothing.

The Buddhist doctrine of rebirth also holds that our future existence after death is strongly conditioned by the ethical nature of our behaviour in this life, with dominant habitual tendencies influencing our future rebirth and development. One could call this the deep implication of natural ethics – that the ethical nature of our actions bring consequences not just for the world we live in, but also for the type of existence we are drawn towards within that world. Our actions help make the world, and also draw us back into it, and into specific aspects of it. The moral nature of our actions doubly affects us, as well as affecting others.

The doctrine of rebirth is to be distinguished from that of reincarnation, which is the theory that there is an unchanging essence, or soul, which goes from life to life. In contrast the doctrine of rebirth is that there is an ever-changing flow of non-physical mental processes which interacts in turn with those physical processes which are our bodies. The doctrine of rebirth is also associated with the fact that each of us is not a separate, unchanging entity, an unchanging self or soul. Indeed, it brings into question what is meant by 'self', and blurs the distinction between self and other.

Conclusion

That all conditioned phenomena are impermanent is a crucial aspect of a Buddhist understanding of the world. Personally, I am very aware, as I have previously mentioned, that positive developments from the western tradition could be lost. Sadly, they could be lost because of the contributory effects of various negative aspects of the western tradition, combined with threats from outside it. As I described in my first chapter, it appears that in the West we are now in an era of profound insecurity. That insecurity is partly due to the ongoing financial crisis, but also due to the associated bankruptcy of dominant ways of thinking deriving from physicalism. In addition, there is much criminal and corrupt practice within business and government around the world.

Added to this situation there has been a revival of what one could call theistic 'revelationism', otherwise known as fundamentalism, with its utterly vicious intolerance, whilst authoritarian state capitalism is also on the rise. An important question is to what extent are democracy and human rights under threat. Are the conditions supportive of them becoming more precarious? Moreover, will there be very serious consequences of climate change which could further undermine the stability of Western societies?

This brings back into focus the fundamental dilemma of the hunter gatherers. Can the human race overcome this, or will it succumb to it as the twenty-first century continues? Can the different groups that make up the human world together overcome the dilemma?

Moreover, the fact that in complex systems there are often no easy solutions also relates especially to the 'fundamental dilemma' and to overcoming it. This dilemma specifically involves trying to guess or work out what another group is going to do. A crucial issue is that, if only one group seriously practices human rights, this may leave it vulnerable to those that willingly violate those rights, or who actively disbelieve in them and consider themselves justified in treating others inhumanely. Have western liberal democracies become vulnerable because of this issue?

In thinking about this I understand that there is a natural morality with respect to group behaviour, and a natural morality of culture, as well as a natural morality of individual human behaviour. Groups and cultures, as well as individuals, can be assessed as to how moral or immoral they are. There is what one could term 'group egotism', which is to be contrasted with healthy group functioning. The latter can be defined as group functioning that encourages and supports the wellbeing of the group members, but not to the serious detriment of other people. Group egotism is group activity that harms others, and also involves any beliefs which justify that group's interests as being above everyone else's. One could call it 'group psychopathy' when that group egotism is enacted in behaviour and beliefs which involve deliberately harming others, totally ignoring their welfare, and viewing them as inferior or intrinsically wicked. There is also what could be termed cultural psychopathy, which is any set of beliefs that reflect and encourage group psychopathy.

However, it must also be acknowledged that one should not simply ignore one's own group, as if it was of no value, and as if everyone else in the world somehow has more rights than members of one's own group. There is a balance to be struck, with the wellbeing of one's own group being seriously considered, whilst keeping in mind the wellbeing of others.

Furthermore, whether one considers individuals or groups, a vital concept is that of duty. Each of us has duties towards other people. Those duties involve behaving ethically. There are no rights without duties, because for one person to have rights implies that others have duties towards them. The UN Declaration of Human Rights actually does mention duty in one clause, although this tends to be forgotten. Often rights come to be seen as entitlements without reciprocal duties being involved. Many a selfish person has emphasised their rights whilst neglecting their duties. However, rights and duties are two sides of the same coin.

Within a group, people have duties towards each other. Within the world as a whole, groups have duties towards each other. The world is a potential community of positively interacting groups, a situation one could term a potential 'culture of healthy mutuality'. To some extent over the last sixty years or so it has developed away from being just a battlefield of warring groups, away from the fundamental dilemma. This development now appears under serious threat. Let us hope that ways forward can be worked out which build upon that development, and which move further towards a culture of healthy mutuality rather than away from it.

Notes and references

Chapter 1

1. Peter Mair; Ruling the Void; Verso, 2013
2. Francis Fukuyama; The End of History and the Last Man; Penguin, 1992
3. Shorter Oxford English Dictionary
4. John Maynard Keynes; The General Theory of Employment, Interest, and Money; MacMillan, 1936
5. Jean-Martin Charcot, quoted in Henri Ellenberger; The Discovery of the Unconscious, chapter 3, p149 (Fontana edition, 1994)
6. Pierre Janet, quoted in Henri Ellenberger; The Discovery of the Unconscious, chapter 3, p149 (Fontana edition, 1994)

Chapter 2

1. Paul Johnson; A History of Christianity, pp9-16; Penguin, 1982
2. Ibid, Part 2, 'From Martyrs to Inquisitors'; pp67-122;
3. Ibid, Part 2, 'From Martyrs to Inquisitors'; pp67-122;
4. Ibid, pp 117-122
5. Peter Watson; Ideas, A History from Fire to Freud; p333; Phoenix, 2005
6. Ibid, p333
7. Ibid, pp336-338
8. Ibid, pp492-525
9. Ibid, pp492-525
10. Ibid, p500
11. Ibid, pp510-511
12. Paul Johnson; A History of Christianity; pp252-264
13. Peter Watson; Ideas; pp531-550, Phoenix, 2005
14. Richard Tarnas; The Passion of the Western Mind; pp209-211; Pimlico, 2010
15. Peter Watson; Ideas; pp526-550

16. Richard Tarnas; The Passion of the Western Mind; pp211-219; Pimlico, 2010; Peter Watson; Ideas; pp551-574; Phoenix, 2005
17. Peter Watson; Ideas; p290; Phoenix, 2005
18. Cicero; On the Good Life; Trans. Michael Grant; Introduction, pp8-9; Penguin; 1986
19. Paul Johnson; A History of Christianity, pp271-9; Penguin, 1982
20. John Gribbin; The Fellowship; pp3-20; Allen Lane, 2005
21. John Locke; The Second Treatise of Government & A Letter Concerning Toleration; Edited by J.W. Gough; Basil Blackwell, Oxford 1956

Chapter 3

1. Referred to in Sangharakshita; Buddhism, World Peace and Nuclear War; Windhorse Publications, 1984
2. *Karaniyamettasutta; Sutta Nipata 1.8*
3. Steve Pinker; The Better Angels of Our Nature; Allen Lane, 2011
4. UN Declaration of Human Rights
5. A.C. Grayling; Towards the Light; pp244-5; Bloomsbury, 2008
6. A. Arblaster; The Rise and Decline of Western Liberalism; Blackwell, 1986
7. Rowan Williams; Freedom and Slavery; Wilberforce Lecture Trust; 2007
8. Gertrude Himmelfarb; The Roads to Modernity; Vintage, 2005
9. Sangharakshita; The Individual, The Group and the Spiritual Community; Sadhana Press, 1986
10. e.g. "The community is a fictitious body…"; Jeremy Bentham; Introduction to the Principles of Morals and Legislation", chapter 1; 1780
11. *Culahatthipadopamasutta*; Lesser Discourse on the simile of the elephant's footprint; *Majjhima Nikaya*

Chapter 4

1. Paul Krugman; How did economists get it so wrong? New York Times; Sept 2nd, 2009
2. Norman Hampton; The Enlightenment; p101; Penguin, 1990
3. Adam Smith; The Wealth of Nations, Book IV, Chapter 2.
4. J. Bentham; Principles of Morals and Legislation; Chapter 1; 1780
5. H. Spencer; First Principles, section 97; Williams & Norgate, 1867
6. R. Nadeau; Neoclassical Economic Thinking; The Encyclopedia of Earth
7. S. Jevons; Theory of Political Economy. Chapter 1, paragraph 4; MacMillan 1888
8. Let us suppose that the utility of an object could be given a number, 'two utility units' for example, although this in itself is highly debatable. Technically, using the terminology of 'abstract algebra', the set of such possible 'numbers' for utility *might* amount to being a 'partial ordering' - in other words a set of 'numbers' or, at least, labels, where each can be considered less than or greater than at least some of the others. But that is all, at best. What cannot be assumed is that one can define mathematical operations on this set of labels, operations such as addition. Without being able to apply mathematical operations on them one cannot use the calculus, which is dependent upon the applicability of such operations, as well as other conditions.
9. E. Reinert; Civilising Capitalism; Real World Economic Review, Issue 63, March 2013
10. R. Hofstadter; Social Darwinism in American Thought; Beacon Press, 1955; G. Jones; Social Darwinism and English Thought; The Harvester Press, 1980
11. Hegel, quoted in O. Chadwick; The Secularization of the European Mind in the Nineteenth Century; pp131-133; Cambridge University Press, 1977
12. J.B. Lamarck; Wikipedia article
13. Malthus T.R.; 1798. *An essay on the principle of population.* Oxford World's Classics

14. G. Jones; Social Darwinism and English Thought; Chapter 6
15. Joseph Sottile: The Fascist Era: Imperial Japan and the Axis Alliance in Historical Perspective (Prepared for the Association for Asian Studies Conference Washington, D.C., April 4-7, 2002)
16. K. Marx & F. Engels; Manifesto of the Communist party; Progress Publishers, Moscow 1973, p 59 & p76
17. D Ricardo; Principles of Political Economy and Taxation, chapter 1; 1817
18. K Marx & F. Engels; ibid; p58 & p66
19. C. Guevara; El Paredon

Chapter 5

1. Herbert Spencer, First Principles; section 60; Williams & Norgate, 1867
2. F. Edgeworth; Mathematical Psychics; p9 & p12, Kegan Paul & Co., 1881
3. Baron D'Holbach; System of Nature, 15; 1770
4. 'Comte, Positivism and the Religion of Humanity'; www.victorianweb.org
5. O. Chadwick; The Secularization of the European Mind in the Nineteenth Century; Ch7; Cambridge University Press, 1977
6. C.S. Hall; A Primer of Freudian Psychology; p 12; Mentor Books, 1954
7. K. & W. Hopper; The Puritan Gift; I.B. Tauris, 2007
8. Ibid, pp216-219
9. Ibid, Chapter 11
10. O. Chadwick; The Secularization of the European Mind in the Nineteenth Century; p237; Cambridge University Press
11. J. Searle; Rediscovering the Mind; Introduction; MIT Press, 1992
12. D. Dennett; Kinds of Minds, Phoenix, 1997; Chapter 2, p31
13. T. Metzinger; The Ego Tunnel, chapter 3; Basic Books, 2009

14. e.g. U. Place; 'Is Consciousness a Brain Process?' in J. O'Connor (Ed.), Modern Materialism; Readings on Mind Body Identity; Harcourt, Brace and World, 1969

Chapter 6

1. E. Heidbreder; Seven Psychologies; Prentice-Hall; chapter 3; 1933
2. Ibid; chapter 4
3. Ibid; chapter 7
4. H. Ellenberger; The Discovery of the Unconscious; Fontana, 1994
5. C.S. Hall: 'A Primer of Freudian Psychology', Mentor Books, 1954
6. C.S. Hall: ibid; p15
7. A. Beck et al.; Cognitive Therapy of Depression; Guilford, 1979
8. A. Watts; Psychotherapy East and West; Pantheon Books, 1961
9. E. Fromm, D. Suzuki & De Martino; Zen Buddhism and Psychoanalysis; Souvenir Press, Harper & Brothers, 1960
10. Padmasiri Da Silva; Buddhism and Psychoanalysis; Lake House, 1973
11. Edwin Arnold; The Light of Asia; Windhorse Publications
12. Lama Govinda; Foundations of Tibetan Mysticism; Rider, 1969
13. re Hakomi therapy: see www.hakomi.com
14. re Core Process Psychotherapy: see www.karuna-institute.co.uk
15. J. Kabat-Zinn; Full Catastrophe Living; Piatkus, 2013
16. M. Linehan; Cognitive Behavioural Treatment of Borderline Personality Disorder; Guilford Press, 1993
17. Z. Segal, JM.G. Williams & J. Teasdale; Mindfulness Based Cognitive Therapy for Depression; Guilford Press, 2002
18. e.g. Lisa Kilpatrick et al; Impact of mindfulness based stress reduction training on intrinsic brain connectivity; NeuroImage 56 (2011) pp290-298
19. e.g. (1) 'Meditation gives brain a charge, study finds', by Marc Kaufman, Washington Post, Jan 3rd 2005; referring to the work of Richard Davidson; (2) Maria Ergstrom and Birgitta Solderfeldt; Brain

activation during compassion meditation, a case study; J. Alternative and complementary medicine, 16,5 2010, pp597-599
20. Padmal Da Silva; Buddhism and Behaviour Change; in Beyond Therapy, ed. Guy Claxton; Wisdom Publications, 1986
21. John Bowlby; Attachment and Loss; Basic Books, 1969
22. e.g. Scientific American Mind, Vol 23, issue 9; Wisdom from Psychopaths?
23. Thich Nhat Hanh; Transformation and Healing; Sutra on the four establishments of mindfulness, p29; quoted in 'The Buddha's radical path of jhana', by Bodhipaksha, www.wildmind.org:

'The Four Form Jhānas and the Four Formless Jhānas are states of meditational concentration which the Buddha practiced with teachers such as Ālāra Kālāma and Uddaka Rāmaputta, and he rejected them as not leading to liberation from suffering. These states of concentration probably found their way back into the sutras around two hundred years after the Buddha passed into mahāparinirvāna. The results of these concentrations are to hide reality from the practitioner, so we can assume that they shouldn't be considered Right Concentration.' (Transformation and Healing: Sutra on the Four Establishments of Mindfulness, page 29)

Chapter 7

1. Sangharakshita; A Survey of Buddhism; Tharpa Publications, Chapter 1, section 11. & Sangharakshita; The Three Jewels; Windhorse Publications, chapter 12
2. N. Johnson; Two's Company, Three is Complexity; Oneworld Publications; 2007 & N. Boccara; Modelling Complex Systems; Springer, 2004
3. W.B. Arthur; Inductive Reasoning and Bounded Rationality; American Economic Review (Papers and Proceedings) 84, 406-411, 1994; 'El Farol Bar problem'; Wikipedia;
4. 'Tulip Mania'; Wikipedia

5. I. Newton; Philosophiae Naturalis Principia Mathematica; Project Gutenberg

6. Maxwell's equations imply that light waves cannot be 'standing waves', i.e. waves which at any given point in space remain the same. This is because light is an electromagnetic wave which has two components, an electric field and a magnetic field. In a light wave, at any given point in space the value of each field is proportional to the rate of change, with time, of the other field at that point. If there is no rate of change of either field at any given point, as in a standing wave, then the value of each field is zero. If one were travelling along at light speed beside the light wave, then in one's frame of reference it would appear to be a standing wave. But then that would mean it does not exist.

7. A. Einstein; 'On the Electrodynamics of Moving Bodies'; 1905, translated in 'Einstein's Miraculous Year'; J. Stachel, editor; Princeton, 1998

8. D. Lawden; An Introduction to Tensor Calculus and Relativity; Chapter 6; Methuen, 1971

9. A. Aczel; Entanglement; Chapter 3; Wiley, 2003

10. R. Feynman; 'QED, The Strange Story of Light and Matter'; Penguin, 1985, p9:

'Why are you going to sit here all this time, when you won't be able to understand what I am going to say? It is my task to convince you not to turn away because you don't understand it. You see, my physics students don't understand it either. That is because I don't understand it. Nobody does."

11. M. Peskin & D. Schroeder; An Introduction to Quantum Field Theory; Westview, 1995

12. Martin Rees, Astronomer Royal; Prospect, May 2012, p72

13. The Flower Ornament Scripture (*Avatamsaka Sutra*), Volume 1, Book Five: 'The Flower Bank World', p223; Translated by Thomas Cleary; Shambala, 1985

Chapter 8

1. Kenneth & William Hopper; The Puritan Gift; Chapters 11 & 12; I.B. Tauris, 2007
2. Ibid; Chapter 12
3. Nicholas Timmins; The Chief Executive's Tale; Kings Fund, May 2016
4. For example, extreme feminism embodies this pattern, portraying men in a highly prejudiced and hateful manner. Thus: "The common erotic project of destroying women makes it possible for men to unite into a brotherhood; this project is the only firm and trustworthy groundwork for cooperation among males and all male bonding is based on it." (Andrea Dworkin; www.brainyquote.com) Such statements parallel Marxist pronouncements about the bourgeoisie, and also Nazi propaganda against Jewish people.
5. European Framework National Statute for the Promotion of Tolerance:
http://www.europarl.europa.eu/meetdocs/2009_2014/documents/libe/dv/11_revframework_statute_/11_revframework_statute_en.pdf
6. Herbert Marcuse; Repressive Tolerance; 1965; http://www.marcuse.org
7. John Rawls; Theory of Justice, p12; Harvard University Press, 2005
8. Jim B. Tucker; Return to Life; St. Martin's Griffin, 2013

www.ingramcontent.com/pod-product-compliance
Ingram Content Group UK Ltd.
Pitfield, Milton Keynes, MK11 3LW, UK
UKHW021051270726
13967UKWH00012B/567